To
Penn Hills
Library

Thanks for your
support

Class of 82
Debra Clark

Everyone Has A Story

Printed in the United States of America

First Printing, 2015

Front Cover photography by John W. McDonough
Back Cover photo by Deborah Norrell

Index

There are so many people that I would like to thank and should you've played a part in some manner please do not be offended if I forgotten to mention you. This project has taken me some time to get out, and I might have forgotten someone in the process...I would like to thank my new church home Covenant Church of Pittsburgh Pa for their great love, support and most of all helping me get truly set FREE! My accountant Loretta Carter who turned my finances around after a extremely long divorce and rode me to the grocery store when I couldn't afford a vehicle (yes it got that bad) and those times you learn who your friends are. And two of my praying sister's in Christ, Sherry from Louisiana and Lorita Kelsey Childress, who believe in this project so much that she told me that I would someday be on "Black Girls Rock"! And to my Aunt Juanita, thank you for all of the encouragement in the mid-night hour. To my mother who gave me life and tried her best to make it abundant, she came a close second to God. To my siblings Stanley, Lisa and Holly you all showed me love when I needed and were my first sparring partners so I learned how to survive in a sometimes very cruel world...I gave my opponents hell until I met Jesus. And to the loves of my life in this world my two children who I just adore and so grateful that God placed you in my life to make the journey a little easier when things got rough! You two were my very inspiration to get this completed, for a good woman leaves an inheritance to her children and her children's children, I know you will govern over it with Wisdom. And to my Lord and Savior Jesus the Christ you are and forever will be my Rock, your loving sister Debra.

I would like to dedicate this book to two of my friends who's stories were told in the media. Nicole Brown Simpson who I met on a few occasions through my relationship with Jim Brown and my friend Beth Anne Anderson who helped give me my first baby shower and later I got to return her the favor, the only difference is that she knew my daughter and I never got to meet hers They were all murdered by Beth Anne's boyfriend 2 weeks after Melonie was born along with Beth Anne's son Kevin. They too were featured in the media"America's Most Wanted". They all gave me the courage to tell mine, as the title said..."Everyone has a Story"!

You never know what is going to be your source of strength or even where it would come from. I always wanted to get this out, but timing never seemed to be right. Today I learned that those are distractions from the enemy to prevent one from living out their purpose in life. I wanted to protect my children from hearing about my past, it seemed too complicated for young children. Not knowing that they could learn from my mistakes and how to avoid trouble in their lives. I began this project when I was going through another tough time in my life…divorce! I started to journal only to see my life on paper in front of me to see if I could locate any patterns in order to learn something. Divorce never frighten me. I had gone through it before as a child, but I knew what it may do to my children. Not knowing how the other party may react could complicate the matter even more. Actually I have to say thank you to my ex for all of the aggravation, turning desperation into inspiration! Hopefully putting my book on the "Best Sellers" list!, and help women over come their fears of leaving an abusive man and dare to live their lives as if it's the only one that they were given!

Jim Brown once told me that everyone who wrote a book about their life story generally aren't any good, because they don't they don't have the balls to tell the truth and nothing but the truth. But this is what I've come to learn…yea shall know the truth and the truth shall make you free, and I am free indeed! Thank you Lord.

CHAPTER ONE

I have always started things out with a bang (literally and figuratively). Well this time it was literally! At Sunset Plaza Drive in the middle of the night I would fire off five to six rounds of bullets into the air. Until I heard someone say…"Drop that weapon", and I thought …"What weapon"?! That would be the first time that I would have an outer body experience. My therapist called it "shock" and today I know it was a combination to both.

I was surrounded by the L. A. P. D. I can't tell you just how many. It was dark and I had just experienced something that never happened to me before in my life. I was beaten by a man who was three times my size and more than twice my age. My house guest Doreen was holding on to me and I was holding on to Jim's 45 revolver that just jammed before the police arrived. Before that night I had only seen a gun one time in my life, but had never held one. But I certainly knew that if I'd pick one up I would use it. That was the advice I got early in life from my father.

I don't recall if the police had guns drawn on me it was dark and I was in shock. It seemed as if they had seen this before. They knew that I was in trouble and they were there to help. One of the officers would come over to me and genteelly remove the gun from my hands and wrap his arms around me. He knew I had been through a great ordeal. Others were questioning Doreen and Denise who was awakened by the police's flashlights in her face. They had taken us in different directions, which is police procedure to make sure our stories added up. As the officer was walking me down the curved driveway I noticed them standing around and holding down the NFL Great Jim Brown. Well, he didn't look so great then, begging me for his forgiveness and pleading for mr to tell the police this was all a big mistake. He was still wearing his grey terry cloth pool wrap and nothing else. He was face down on the ground with his hands handcuffed behind his back. The only mistake that was made that night was that I was a terrible shot and I didn't leave him permanently. I had more to experience, but it came with a price that I wasn't able to pay. To whom much is given, much is required…

CHAPTER TWO

It was Harlem in the 1960's. The place I was born and full of diversity. A place where African Americans were free, and made a name for them selves. A Black Mecca! You could be what ever your heart desired anything from a "Pimp" to a "Business Man". Heck most pimps were business men! My neighborhood consist of everything…doctors, judges, lawyers, dry cleaners. Every thing one needed you could fine right inside Harlem! They were proud successful men from all sorts of back grounds. A time where black men were still involved with their families and communities. I was in awe of them all. I always had a thing for my own men of color. I hailed from an "Historical Black Family" full of strong black leaders! Which came naturally to me to be supportive of black men as a whole. They possessed a confidence and swag no other race of men had. I guess that is one of the reasons why that term says…"once you go black" comes from. The only thing I didn't like was the way some of them dressed being I came from such distinguished men. Men like Nicky Barns who dressed too colorful for my taste, however I respected his right to do so. I remember another drug dealer Frank Lucas who just looked like a business man in a well tailored suit. Well, he was. He just did things differently. Somehow I was mature enough to see them in as individuals. I knew it was more to everyones story. That people have many layers to them and not to judge. If I simply looked at myself I was a good girl, but if you'd pushed me around too hard, I could be your worst nightmare! I knew if a person was honest with themselves they had good and bad in them, and just needed the wrong thing to bring the bad out.

My mother met my father when my she got pregnant during her senior year in High School. I believe it was kept a tight knit secret among her family. She was shipped to New York to her maternal Aunt June who was a nurse to either have the baby away from prying eyes or the second to get rid of it because of the connections Aunt June had at a hospital. Aunt June knew of doctors who would perform those types of surgeries. They had the ability to make it go away (it being my mothers pregnancy). Then she could return to her life in Pittsburgh without tainting her families reputation. I choose to believe that it was the first. In the process she met my father and he instantly fell in love with her. My mother was a "knock out"! She had a killer body which was all of her own (people didn't get plastic surgery in those days) you either had it or you didn't. Thick hair that past the middle of her back and big beautiful eyes with a very king nose money couldn't buy! Carmel complexion and had the nerve to be a lingerie' model even though she was pregnant. That's the beauty of youth, you can look great under most circumstances. It takes time or a lot of trauma to damage that kind of beauty. I thank God my mother met my father and had her own mind or non of us might have gotten here. He had great character and married my mother at a judges home up state New York. He then adopted my brother as soon as he was born and never said a word about this to his dying day. I went almost my entire life before I learned my brother had a different father. I thought that was very noble of my father and in return my mother gave him Lisa. Lisa was born in Feb 14,1962. A Valentine's Day gift of sorts. There were two terrible things that would occur with her birth, one being she was born premature and needed a blood transfusion, and the other terrible thing, is that when my mother gave birth to her it left my mother paralyzed. I believe that all of the changes that my mother endured in such a short amount of time caused her body to break down. My mother stayed in the hospital for 9 months. Praise God for my grand mother Daisy Clark. She was what most African American people had in their families. She was "Big Mama". She only had a third grade education, however there are some things that aren't taught in class. She had common sense and most people know that common sense isn't common! Daisy never met a challenge that she couldn't handle or fix. She had grace to walked through any amount of adversity. Funny thing that I remember about her is that she would hum and make up words to gospel songs as she went. She never seemed to have enough money but would go play a number as if she were going off to work and by faith she would come back with her winnings and made a lot of things happen with that money. Everyone in the community loved and respected her. Even the drug addicts and dope pushers in the community. When she walked down the block everyone spoke or even tipped their hats. When she walked in tight spaces they would even part like the "Red Sea" to let her through. She would take Lisa home with her to join my brother Stanley and the rest of my cousins along with my fathers younger brother Noble and his new bride, my feisty Porto Rican Aunt Santa. My poor mother would be in that hospital for the next nine months. Daisy held down the fort, but she also knew that her son wasn't being the strength that his family needed. She tried to supplement but she knew there are somethings that only a man could do. He had to learn how to be strong for his wife and children. Even though he tired his hardest, somehow he couldn't seem to do what was right or good enough for my mother. Even though my mother always described him as very intelligent. He studied mathematics and received a full scholarship to college which was a big feet for a black youth in the late 1950's. Yet, he choose other sources of employment for fast money and to take care of his wife and family. Most of his hustle was in local bars. There was gambling and the exchanging of many sorts of illegal activity which was very lucrative and common place in large cities. Not so much for my mothers background. My father knew that my mother wasn't knowledgeable of this type of life style, so he kept most of his activities away from her and where it was excepted in the streets. At first he was a good provider and my mother later learned that he claimed his siblings on his tax returns and that was their first financial set back. All of his earnings were taken by the IRS. So my mother took employment at a bank and being very beautiful living in New York, modeling jobs came easily. It caused problems between the two of them. My father was old school and no wife of his was going to work outside the home. Besides, they now had two children and he wanted her at home. However, my mother was going to see to it that they weren't going to go without. She wasn't ready to throw in the towel. She was accustomed to having nice things and wanted for us to have the same things she had as a child.

My father still went to work, but under the table type of work. He still managed bars and to my mother, it seemed as if he were having too much fun. She wanted him to have a more respectable job, much like her grand father and great grand father "The Rev. Dr. William Hooper Councill Esq"., founder of Alabama A&M University and much more. It would be like comparing the President to a janitor. That is why one shouldn't compare, he could never live up to her standard. Well, for now it wasn't a thing she could do…she was going to keep working and not allow her family to find out just how bad her decision making had gotten her.

Once my mother was released from the hospital Daisy insisted that she stay in that already crowded 3 bed room apartment. She knew that my mother couldn't return home with a toddler and now 9 month old baby. My father kept long hours at the bar and was appearing stressed as if he knew his ways were the cause of my mother's health issues. He was partially right. I don't think most men could have lived up to my mothers or her families high expectations. She just had a very unique up bring. She was raised by her grand parents Dr. Walter Solomon Buchanan (First President of Alabama A&M University and a Harvard graduate class of 1907). He was also a promenade business man that rivaled even men of the white race. She grew up very pampered!

What I learned in life there are many layers to all people and because my parents lives were so different, they seemed to be doomed from the start. They simply were not equally yoked. But they needed to meet. They shared a purpose in their meeting. They had to bear children. All of whom would have a purpose.

I don't know if it were all of the chaos that went on in my grand mothers three bedroom apartment that gave life to my mothers weak little body, or the chaos put fire under her feet to get well and get the heck out of there. Either way she got better and moved us back
to our apartment.

Many of my mothers friends would come by to help out and so many days a week Daisy would march herself up to see what was going on and to help out. My father even stepped up for a while. He wasn't afraid to be hands on, he was the eldest of seven siblings. Changing of diapers and making breakfast was his thing, since he was out most nights working when he got off it was morning and now time for breakfast. My mother said that a lot of the times he came home in the morning he was still drunk. She would lye in the bed and listen to him talk and change Lisa's diaper and make oatmeal for Stanley. At times she enjoyed it and others not so much. She knew that his behavior wouldn't be excepted by her family and wasn't sure how she continue to hide her life in New York without anyone from her family finding out. When she was feeling much better, she and her friend Zenobia would go and visit my father at the bar. He wasn't happy about it but knew she needed to get out of the house and that was a way for them to see each other. They must have still had an attraction towards each other because by the time my mother went for a check up she was pregnant with baby number three.

This wasn't good news for her from her doctor. He warned against it and my father was even on the doctors side. He told my mother we could always have more children later, but now wasn't the time and he wasn't willing to risk the possibly of her becoming paralyzed again. Here's the thing…she was already 6 months along in her pregnancy! All that they could do was pray and wait. God was good and I came out a healthy 7 pounds with every thing in tact and so was my mother. To this day she said that I was her easiest birth and easiest to raise. God knew that they needed a break or just maybe I wouldn't have made it here. For a while my mother accepted her life and most women know one can loose track of time raising children Her routine was cooking cleaning and if she were lucky someone would stop by and give her a break.

I was turning two, so my mother planned a small party for me. To this very day she didn't understand how I remembered it in such detail. I wore a light blue dress with short sleeves with white ruffles around the neck and bottom of my dress. Fabrics in those days were ruff and stiff to the touch. It irritated my new skin and itched terribly. My mother hadn't noticed she had her hands full with keeping my cousins calm so she could set things up. They were excited to have cake and ice-cream which was a treat that my grand mother couldn't always afford. It was enough for her to keep meals on the table. We were all cramped into my parents small kitchen, and I was sitting on top of the kitchen table with news paper underneath me for any spills. My mother was always thinking ahead much like me today, I guess that is where I get that from. The second thing that I remembered was the cake. It was a yellow battered rounded two layered cake with white icing and coconut shavings between the layers and outside of the cake. The reason I remember so well is that the coconut shavings irritated my gums where I hadn't yet grown teeth. Much like a poppy seed would be to a person who wore dentures. God bless my mother for trying, she had a lot on her plate. Especially coming from such a privilege back ground. It's a miracle she didn't crack up under those strained circumstances. She went from having grown up with maids and governess to cooking and cleaning for a family of five in a few years time all by herself. Even though she had those things, she also told me that she wasn't so privilege where she didn't have chores. Nevertheless, I am sure this isn't what she had in mind.

Again my mother would see the same patterns in my fathers behavior. She would listen to him talk to me (much like he did with Lisa) when he changed my diapers and gave me a bottle. She said that I would lay there in bowels up my back and just kick and cooed as if nothing ever bothered me! She was becoming more tired of his late nights and drinking, but now had the three children to support. Even though she got a few breaks in-between it was enough to insure a future for her and her children. What possibly could my father secure for us?! He wasn't a respectful business man and didn't share her same back ground. Her doubts of keeping us in the city she now parlayed into a plan of action. Because things were changing in Harlem and drugs were causing so much chaos, I am sure that was the dividing factor she made to put her plan into action. She made a call to her mother and Aunt Lois (who assisted in raising her), they would drive up to New York and come to take us all back to Pittsburgh…every one of us except my father.

In the spring of 1967 my mother made her move. My brother said that he would never forget the day that we left New York. He described the cries that came from my father sounded like a wounded animal in the wild! He said that his last view of our father he was laying on the side walk screaming and moaning in emotional torment.

My maternal grand mother (Helen) and her new husband Allen Walker, who was a very large man, mostly loaded up everything in our apartment and we all drove off. The way my brother described that day I am glad that I had no remembrance of it. Funny thing, I could remember my birthday party.

CHAPTER THREE

Even though my grand mother Helen brought us back, we weren't going to stay with them. My grand mother Helen had a new life with her new husband Allen. They had two new children of their own Allen Jr. (aka Mighty) and a daughter Verda. They weren't much older then my mothers children, just a few years between them and my brother Stanley. Explains why my grand mother hadn't been up to see about things in New York, she too had her hands full. Come to find out not much of my mothers family were around. Most were dying off while she was having us. It seems that's what God does, replaces what He takes.

Well, we would move into the house of my now late Uncle Councill Buchanan. He was my grand father's eldest brother. My uncle was named after the founder of Alabama A&M University (Rev. Dr. William Hooper Councill Esq). Now I know why my father felt so antiquate! Just generations of accomplished men. My Uncle Councill's widow was still alive my (Aunt Lois Buchanan) she was Psychiatrist and had multiple degrees from Duquesne University. They didn't have any children and were the last members in the Buchanan Clan to raise my mother when many members of our family was dying out. And because of her strict ways, she was probably the reason my mother got pregnant having to secretly go out for a little fun. Fortunately for us my mother gave us much more freedom probably because she wished that she'd been given some. My mother was proud of her families accomplishments non the less, however they all had great hopes for my mother to have follow in their footsteps. Lois and my grand father's baby sister Ida Christine Buchanan-Chamberlin both worked with the real Sibble (the woman they made a movie about staring Sally Fields). Nevertheless Aunt Lois was probably glad to have us as a new project, after loosing her husband and having no children of their own. She welcomed us back with open arms. My mother knew there was a change in Lois, she was drinking heavily. At night when Lois was drinking she would keep my mother up talking about what she thought my mother should do with all of these children. She knew that my Aunt Christine had charge over most of what was left of our families estate, and now Aunt Christine had her own family and they would be her first priority. Much of the other parts of the estate were confiscated by the state of Alabama. She couldn't perceive just how my mother would make it…heck neither did my mother, however she would take it one day at a time.

Well, word got around that Little Charlotte was back in town and the men were lining up. My mother always had a great sense of humor and larger than life spirit and personality! She had me at 23 and now about 26 still in her prime! Not like today where people eat a lot of fast food mostly for convience. Since there wasn't much of that at that time, it made it a lot easier for a woman to keep their figure. My Aunt Lois's drinking and criticism of my mother again put fire under her feet to get us our own place and so my mother found us the cutest little 3 bed room ranch house right in her mother (Helen's) neighborhood of North Versailles P.A. It was a modest neighborhood but very well maintained. Mostly of African Americans who held jobs at a near by steel mill. That was were Helens husband Allen worked.

Well, Hallelujah Charlotte had her very own place and freedom. Our furniture looked really nice there. We were happy and too young to miss my father yet and so busy seeing everyone and getting acclimated with two moves in such a short amount of time. North Versailles seemed to be a better fit for children. A lot of fresh air, tree's and outdoors. We had room to rip and run around. My brother Stanley loved it. Behind our house was a wooded area with exploration fit for any young boy. Stanley was in heaven. Not so much for me and Lisa, because our yard had no fence, which made my mother keep close tabs on us. I was just a few month's shy of turning 3. We had settled down and was attending our local church(Mt.Carmel Baptist) and life seemed to be good! My mother had a suitor who came around and made sure she had transportation of her own. His name was Ralph Robinson.

He knew my mother long before she moved to New York, but he knew my mother was only separated but still stuck around. He thought of himself as some sort of "Play Boy" and seemed happy that she was still married, so he wouldn't have to be honorable and marry her. I don't believe that my mother would have married him even if he were single. She always called him "Promise Robinson", because he made promises he never kept. She was much smarter than that! Well, he wasn't the only one who got in that line to date her. Plenty of suitors were cutting grass and repairing things around the house, taking us for ice creme what ever they could do get in her good graces. However my mother spent most of her time taking care of us and catching up with her mom and new siblings. But my mother had her hands full. Her sister Verda came down a lot and seemed to be a little envious of my mothers return. She even seemed to envy us. We had custom furniture made from "Bloomingdales" and other high end stores. The best of everything New York had to offer. My mother had great taste. Some times her little sister became problematic for her to be around. But for my big brother Stanley, our little neck of the woods was full of adventure for him. Every morning after a hearty breakfast Stanley would set out for the woods behind our home with our new dog (Highlife). Yes, named after the beer. Highlife was a German Shepard who was a protector. He would follow not only Stanley but us girls as well. It was good for us to have him in our lives for many reasons to come.

One day in particular Stanley was on one of his daily hunts. My mother had purchased a wooden riffle that had a cork stopper connected to a string that was tied to the end of the riffle, so when you fired the gun, the stopper would pop out like a pretend bullet. One day while Stanley was out hunting he ran across a rabbit that was already injured by either another animal or some type of wire fencing. Stanley was in a state of panic. He thought he shot the rabbit with his wooden fake riffle. He picked up the rabbit by it's ears and he and Highlife brought the rabbit home for my mother to fix. Some of the things that she did for the sake of her children still amazes me. Especially since I became a mother. Well, she laid some news paper down on the kitchen table, got some cotton swabs, peroxide and a needle and thread. Well, Dr. Charlotte went to work on that poor little rabbit. She first dissolved an aspirin on a spoon and filled an eye dropper with the solution and fed it to the rabbit for its pain before her next step. Well, I was barely tall enough to see what was going on. My nose had just made it to the surface of the kitchen table while standing on my tippy toes. I was holding my breath waiting to see what was next. She proceeded to clean out the rabbits injury with the cotton and peroxide and then with amazement my mother stitched up that rabbit with a sewing needle and thread. What moxie! She told Stanley to go into her closet and bring her one of her shoe boxes, he ran as fast as he could. She gave each of us some news paper and instructed us to tear it up into little pieces. What?, I thought , she wanted us to make a mess?! She had her reasons for everything....she proceeded to put the shreds of news paper inside the shoe box for the rabbit to rest in while he was healing. Oh my gosh, my mother to me was God himself! I was convinced and would think that much of her for years to come. For the next few days we took turns feeding and caring for that rabbit, mostly Stanley. First it looked as if the rabbit was getting better, he would hop around the shoe box but not well enough to hop very far. One day Stanley woke up to find that the rabbit had died. This crushed all our little souls, but not my mother...she told us to put on our shoes and she put the lid on that shoe box, took us outside and dug a hole and proceeded to give that rabbit the best funeral that we ever seen! She was the most creative mom anyone could have...

Another one of Stanley's adventures might not have ended well if it weren't for our dog Highlife. Stanley was out back and what he thought was a simple gardening snake, he proceeded to pick it up and my mother heard the frantic sounds of our dog barking she knew that it was something more serious. It turned out to be a Copperhead snake, one of the most deadly and poisons snakes around. My mother quickly grabbed a metal shovel and she and Highlife fought that snake and WON! She chopped off the head with her shovel. My mother was something else. That time we were covered. We had a neighborhood girl come by from time to time. Most of the teenage girls admired my mother. She didn't look much older than them. They thought she was somehow just playing house. My mother would let the neighbor girl come by and try some of my mothers fancy things on and sometimes she ate lunch with us. One time she asked my mother if she could take us for a walk, so she did. I am not sure if she had sinister ways or just plain stupid, but she put me and my sister Lisa in a stroller with me up front. She took us up our very steep hill and let go of the stroller racing as fast as it can to the bottom of the street. In the process I was slipping out, my poor little right leg slipped through the opening of the stroller and dragged pulling my skin clean off. It was more than a brush burn, it exposed my flesh down to the white meat. Our dog was chasing the roller and barking until we came to a stop. That's when my mother ran out of the house and like that rabbit she patched me up as well!

Well, from then on we weren't going with anyone else and our world got confined back to just our back yard. My mothers sister Verda would be the only child that was still allowed to play with us. She and Stanley got this bright idea to make a sliding board out of some scraps of wood and other materials. They kept riding and I wanted a turn. As I slid down the makeshift sliding board I caught my tongue on a nail that was sticking out. Well, this time I had to be rushed to the hospital, my tongue was cut half off. There was nothing the hospital could do for my tongue but to use this metal gadget which looked like an old fashioned barrette to hold my tongue together while it healed. I don't remember just how long I had to wear it. I just remember that I couldn't talk for a very long time. That was fine by me I had my big sister Lisa who did all the talking for me, besides I got to eat all of my favorite thing for a very long time (pudding, ice-cream, mashed potatoes and jello). That's a fun diet for a two year old.

I know that my mothers nerves had to be shaken by this point and kept a much closer watch on us. She immediately took down that sliding board and removed all of the parts out of our yard. There seemed to be patterns developing that one can only see with a Spiritual eye. It was a sunny day in March. We started out for church and came home for diner. My mother let us play in the back yard until she was finished warming it up. She instructed us not to get dirty being like most churches we would return for evening service. My mothers sister Verda came by and since my mother was multi tasking like usual on the phone and heating up diner. Verda came over and my mother told her that we were out back. Well, Verda got some bright idea, she wanted to burn the trash in our trash barrel. She went in the kitchen and retrieved the matches off the stove where my mother kept them. Since my mother caught Verda and took the matches from her and told her that she wasn't allowed to use them and to go back out side. For some reason or another my mother slipped out of the kitchen for a few seconds (this is why you'd can never take your eyes off of children not even for a minuet). Verda was watching through the kitchen window and slipped in when my mother wasn't around and took the matches with her outside without my mother noticing. Verda lit the drum and because of the wind and it was very sunny outside, it made it hard to see the flames. At the time I don't know if it was because I had just gotten hurt and knew to get out of harms way or God spared me or it was someone else's time to get hurt. Today I do not believe in coincidences, there was something sinister about where we lived. More like generational curses. Why did these things keep occurring? I had good parents. Lisa was standing too close to the drum and I kept backing up until I got to the door of the house. Our dog was barking like a mad dog which got my mothers attention. Before she could hang up the phone, and back then no 911, she told whom ever she was on the phone with to call for emergency Lisa was on fire! Lisa took off running back and forth in our yard with my mother and dog closely on her trail. Our dog Highlife was the first to catch her and dragged her down the dirt hill in our back yard to help put out the fire. My mother was beating the flames on her body not even noticing she was on fire too. An on looking neighbor ran out of their house with a blanket and covered Lisa's lifeless body, they all jumped into his car and raced off to the hospital. It was then my mother noticed that she too was burnt. They were both getting treatment at the same time. The extent of my mothers burns were just to her hands which they wrapped in gauze which made them looked much like boxing gloves. She said that she didn't even feel it. I learned that once you are injured past the white meat of your flesh you've burned past the nerve which was my only hope for Lisa that she wasn't in severe pain. I remember my grand mother Helen staying with me and Stanley which seemed like for ever before I saw my mother. By this time someone had contacted my father in New York. Being only 2 and a half, I wasn't clear what time when he did arrive to see about her. From my mothers anger toward him, and for many years to come I know it wasn't right away. To his defense most men don't hang around after a breakup. He was a broken man after she left town with us, and I know he must have felt a lot of guilt from what happened to Lisa. Eventually he would make his way to Pittsburgh and wasn't of much help. He blamed my mother for this happening to Lisa, he said that if my mother had stayed with him in New York none of this would have taken place. He told my mother "Who is ever going to want her in that condition"!? He didn't know Jesus either…that's who would want her or any of us who ever felt rejection. Heck, he needed Jesus too. My father had come and gone and none of us seemed to care, I just missed my sister. Sometime around my birthday in August 1967 I got the best present ever, I got to go to the hospital to visit her. I was anxious and a little frightened to see her. I didn't know if I'd recognize her or what. It was a very sterol place, no pictures on the wall and that old pea green paint color on the walls. We walked further and further to the end of the hallway and there was a nurses station on my right and to our left a glass room which Lisa had been for the last 5 months. She looked like Lisa and I burst through the doors and climbed into her hospital bed where she was sitting happily waiting for me. When I looked down I was apprehensive about hugging her, I saw her scars and wasn't sure if I hugged her it might cause her pain. Lisa seemed to be in good spirits, she was ordering one other kid around and some of the nurses. With that all around the clock attention Lisa had become somewhat demanding. The nurses didn't seemed to be bothered by her ways, I guess they were glad to know that she survived a tragic experience and had some awful scars to bare and her road to recovery wasn't just in the hospital. The community surrounded my family and mother and was a great deal of help to her. All of her suitors made themselves useful and didn't even care that sometimes they were doing things for my mother at the same time. One might cut the grass while the other was grocery shopping, but Mr Ralph had the duty of assisting my mother during her"Lady's Time of the Month". Let me tell you something when a man changes your pad…he is a keeper. She could do some things now for us and herself, but in the early days of her injury, she needed a lot of help. Lisa made it home before the Holidays. Mr. Ralph rolled out the red carpet for us all. He also did something huge for my mother, he helped her find a new home for new beginnings! High life was held a "Hero" in the local news papers, he too would go with us to our new home. In some way our dog was an Angel who's assignment was to cover and protect us.

A location doesn't necessarily change a problem, however North Versailles was a daily reminder of the terrible things that took place. But not for Lisa, her physical scars had healed but she was now developing new ones (emotional). Out of guilt we all were let her have her way in every thing. She was becoming someone whom I feared. Getting us into trouble if we didn't allow her to have her way in everything and out of guilt my mother just insisted on us complying. She was my play mate and I wanted to get along. I had missed her and wanted to show her that I was glad that she didn't die, but I didn't know if I were able to endure what she was rapidly becoming. But then, no one knew how to handle those things. We weren't attending church like before.

My mother wasn't comfortable in leaving us again, so her new way of having an outing was inviting friends in. She had a few girlfriends who would bring their children over for a Friday evening of fun. We would play upstairs and at least every 10 minuets or so one of the mothers would check on us. If we got too quiet one of them would be right back up the stairs. They just got together and played cards and some times drank beer. Nothing to heavy then, I think if anyone had gone through all of what my mother endured in those few years, they might have become an alcoholic and /or go crazy(that was satans plan), but it didn't work. This particular night my mothers friend Carolyn invited two men that she met through someone. Walter and David, they were two young men that were serving in the Vietnam War. The odds were staked in their favor 2 to 1. There were the four women in total. My mother and her friends Carlene and Carlene's sister Lisette and their friend Carolyn. For the first time in a long time there was so much laughter in our home. We played nicely upstairs and every now and then either we came downstairs to see what the adults were doing or one of the adults would come up to check on us. I remember Walter coming upstairs to use the bathroom, he glanced over in our room to see why we were so quiet, I peeped up to see him and he had the nice smile and said hi. He used the bathroom that was next door to the bed room where Lisa and I shared. Most of the kids were asleep and the adults were gathering them up to take them home. Lisa and I were up and went down into the living room which was in the front of the house to say goodbye. That was went Walter came over to us and was talking to us. I don't know if someone had shared the story of what happened to Lisa but he gravitated to her and asked her if she has a boyfriend playfully. She replied no and Walter asked if he could be her boyfriend and that he had to go away for a little while and when he returned he would take us out someplace nice. We both looked at each other and smiled. I was ok with him showing her more attention somehow I knew that she needed it and he did too. But Walter had a secret…he had a wife and 3 children living in Newark, New Jersey, one of the children wasn't his. He left to see them before he did his last stance in Vietnam. It was months before we'd see him again. Any how school would start and that would keep us pre-occupied.

When Walter returned he and my mother were inseparable. He was handy and could do or fix anything. He even wasn't bad at cooking. He was young strong and tall and extremely good looking. Walter had a stroll that was better then Denzel Washington's. He would take us sled riding in the winter and we'd stay out until our hands and feet hurt from the cold. He would take my hands and warm them up with his then smile and say one more time. He would carry me on his back up the steep hill and ride us down one more time making me forget that I was even cold! When we got indoors he would make us hot chocolate with marshmallows. We all were in LOVE, and his name was Walter Gaines.

By spring we were settled in and not too many sightings of Ralph anymore. Listen up, if you find someone who does it for you and you don't put a ring on them…that is your lost! School was letting out soon and my mother needed surgery for something of the female kind. She enrolled us in "Fresh Air Summer Camp" for a few weeks out of the summer. I didn't want to go. Being home was

fun for us again and we loved being with Walter. She had to lie on
my application. You had to already be 5 years of age to attend this
camp and I wouldn't turn 5 until my birthday at the end of August.
My neighbors Karen and Rae Morgan were going as well, seems like
it should have been fun, but I wanted to stay at home with mommy
and Walter. Nevertheless, off we went and when we arrive there
were bus loads of children from all over. After they checked us in
they divided us up by sex and age categories. I just knew I would
wound up with Lisa and Rae but I didn't. I didn't know anyone in
my cabin and the first night someone stole my favorite new outfit.
She was stupid enough to even wear it the next day. I told one of
my counselors and she did nothing. She asked how did I know it
was my outfit and at 4 years of age who can prove that, so I told
my sister Lisa on our way to the mess hall. Lisa recognized my
outfit and confronted the girl. Lisa was so angry she pushed the
girl around and scared her half to death to where she wet herself
and my new outfit, then tried to give it back. Well, I didn't want an
outfit that someone peed in and from there on I watched my things
closely. I learned to swim that year at camp and would go on to
have more good memories, like roasting marsh mellows and making
smores, and learning new songs that we sang around a camp fire,
just like the ones you see in the movies. I received one letter from
my mother while we were there and funny thing I wasn't missing
her. I was actually having fun. I didn't see my brother much because
they separated the older boys. I was glad to see him when we got
free time at the pool. They food was pretty bad if it weren't for the
hot dogs and sliced peaches I might not have survived. Next thing I
knew it was time to go home…YEA HOME!

I was sure glad to see my mother, once I returned home
that was when it hit me that how much I loved her but it was ok
for me to have independence every once in a while. It was good to
see Walter as well. They both missed my birthday I had turned five
at camp. They even gave me a small celebration while I was there.
I don't think that they even penalized my mother for fudging her

application about my age. The next morning after we got home Walter woke me up and told me we had something to do. He had a surprise for me…I was very eager to see what he had up his sleeve. We were going for a walk and I told him everything that happened at camp, from the girl stealing my clothes and that I learned to swim and very well. He wasn't much of a talker and I made up for lost time from the months that I couldn't from my injury I received from the sliding board. Well, we had walked all the way to East Liberty to Sears and Roebuck's. I got excited because I thought I knew what he was up to. Well, he took me to the toy department. He let me pick out my very own two wheeler bike. It was "Hot Pink" with a white basket with an assortment of daisies on the front of the basket. It had a white leather seat and training wheels. I was in my glory. He paid for the bike and off we went. Back the same direction as we came. However when we got on Larimar Ave Walter took off my training wheels and said if you could learn to swim at 4 you can learn to ride a bike at 5. Even though I was afraid of falling and getting hurt, I knew he would be right there to catch me. He would be the first man that I would trust! By the time we got home I was riding like a pro. My mother was standing out on the front porch when we returned, to her surprise she saw me from far-off and the closer we got to our house she could see that I didn't have training wheels on. When I became a woman I knew that was the "seal on the deal" for her love for that man, he would take us all to higher heights.

On December 31, 1969 my mother and Walter gave birth to my baby sister Holly Joy Gaines. Back in those days people didn't come to see the baby right away. They thought it wasn't good for the baby to be around potential germs. She was a fat baby with rolls every where, kind of fussy too. She didn't look like me and Lisa, or Stanley. Back them I didn't know what to call it, but she was very light completed. Much like a Mariah Carey. We never had discussions about complexion in our household, but the grand mother who raised my mother and that side of the family did. When my maternal grand father came to visit in the spring I over heard him say...now that's more like it. Even though I didn't know what he meant by it, I somehow knew it made me feel funny inside. He wasn't the kind of grand father who bounced you on his knee and gave you candy. He did some times give us money. His father was the first president of Alabama A&M University and my grand father was married to the late great "Dinah Washington", which made it hard to think that he would be color struck. My mother didn't see much of him growing up either. He was a jazz musician and always on the road, that was why she was raised by his parents Dr. Buchanan and Lady Ida Christine Councill-Buchanan. Lady Ida's father was the Founder of Alabama A&M University amongst many other things. My grand father Walter Buchanan Jr., wasn't polished like the other men in our family even though he was cut from the same cloth. He walked on the wild side and liked music, and bars. He wasn't honorable like the rest. Not even like his brothers. He had a sense of entitlement, but what I really didn't like about him is that he was very attracted to dark women but didn't think that they were good enough to bring home, except for "Dinah". She was a much bigger star than he was. I knew he had a type, my grand mother Helen and Dinah looked like they could be sisters except for their noses. Both had very large breast and big eyed beauty's. He was a bit of a jerk and never had to be responsible, but my mother loved the ground he walked on.

With another child in the family things got a little crowded. It was time to move again. This time we would move to Wilkinsburgh, P.A. I was going to first grade and would attend Turner Elementary School. Back then elementary schools only went up to 5th grade. I had a great principle named Mr. Soble. He was caucasian and sort of round. He had a bald head not totally but like Dr. Phil's from TV. He wasn't the typical caucasian man for those days. He seemed to be fair he didn't look at color. He had compassion for all children and I seemed to have favor with him. He saw that I was competitive and liked a challenge. I was good at art and won a contest that we had on safety. I drew a picture of him disciplining a student and he got a kick out of it. My winning art stayed up on the principles door long after I left the school. Also that year my mother would enroll me and my sister Lisa in "Bea Chorales' School of Dance". I LOOOVEEEDDDD it and could hardy wait until Saturdays would come around to attend rehearsal. I was always practicing, seemed as if I couldn't keep still. My elementary school had "Pee Wee" football team and my grand mother Helen's baby brother Art was a assistant coach. He loved sports and coached his son, my cousin Blaine. My mother came up with the bright idea that the team would need a cheerleading squad, so that started my days as a cheerleader for what would be years to come. I enjoyed it because it involved a lot of activities all at once. I could talk, sing, dance, and do acrobats all at the same time. Up to this point Lisa did the same activities that I did, however she wasn't as enthused about it as I was. It was my life, it was the thing that I woke up every morning excited and ready to do. I was always first by the door and rushed breakfast in order to get in the car so I'd be first to get there to get started.

Summer would roll around fast. This time we would go to a parade...I saw my next love. It was becoming a majorette. I saw an African American girl marching in the parade and was instantly inspired and thought that could be ME. Her name was Cindy Petterson and the marching band was "The Wilkinsburg Americanette's" I walked right up to her and asked her how could I join and where did they practice and what time? Bold for someone who was just completed 3rd grade. I just loved activities and sports. I thought it was a bad thing that I had waited until the end of their season to join, but it was a perfect time to learn the choreography. I believed that I was such a quick study and was able to learn everything in one week, however the winter season was to prepare us for the marching season which started in late spring. Nevertheless my mother had plans for us to keep plenty busy for the rest of the summer.

My step fathers family would come to visit. Most of his brothers and mom and her husband Carl. He wasn't their biological father but you'd never know it. My step father like my father was the eldest in his family as well. It was fun having a house full of people besides they were all young attractive and fun to be around. They all enjoyed music and music was something that was always played in our home all the time. Walter has something called a "Real to Real". It was a tape from back in the day that would play music for hours almost like a huge cassette tape. Since his brother Lewis was a big DJ in New Jersey and New York he would bring us all of his latest disco albums. That was a latest craze of music and again I loved to dance. All day was very entertaining. My mother and her new mother in-law would do most of the cooking and the evenings my step father would be in charge of the grill. I hated when they had to leave but learned of the good news before they would depart. My new uncle Ricky and his wife Eleanor were taking me and my sister Lisa with them to New Jersey for a few weeks when they left. My bags were packed and I couldn't wait.

I got the bug for travel fast, as long as I knew I could return to a safe and happy home I was willing to go anywhere. Uncle Ricky and Aunt Eleanor were a very attractive couple and she had a daughter Simone. She was the only child and was extremely excited to have cousins for the summer. They had an apartment in a development that was new with a pool and everything. They both had jobs and went off to work every morning, but gave us instructions on what we were allowed to do. We were obedient children and when we got up in the morning we made ourselves cereal, watched a few cartoons and then headed for the pool. There was a "Life Guard" on duty and we abided by the rules. We met another family a young girl named Tammy and her baby brother. They were younger than I was, about a year. Like us they were latch key kids too. Boy if this were today ALL of these parents would have been locked up. It was a different time. After we swam for the afternoon (the pool shut down for lunch) we walked Tammy

and her brother to their apartment and went in. OMG we had
never seen such disorder. We didn't stay long and Lisa, Simone and
myself went back to Simone's apartment where we were staying.
Her parents would come home from work and we shared our day
over diner. My Uncle Ricky was a much better cook or so I thought
than my Aunt Eleanor. He introduced us to "Italian Hot Dogs",
they were topped with frenchfries sautéed peppers and onions and
topped them off with ketchup yum yum, I still enjoy those to this
very day. That was the first time I had frozen corn on the cob.
I wished that they did have to go to work, I liked having the
comfort of an adult around especially since we had all of those
tragic accidents.

They next day was almost the same as before we would get
up make cereal and this time skipped cartoons and headed for the
pool hoping to see Tammy and her brother. Lisa and I came up
with a plan Simone went along with it. We wanted to do something
nice for Tammy's family, so when we saw her and her brother we
talked them into taking us back to their apartment and cleaning
it up. So all 5 of us left the pool and headed back to Tammy's
apartment and commence to cleaning. We took out trash made beds
cleaned up toys washed dishes and stacked newspapers even dusted.
Boy did it look good. We couldn't hardy wait for her parents to get
home to hear their praises, and for them to see what we had done.
Well, it didn't turn out that way and they were ANGRY! They yelled
at Tammy four letting us in their apartment and going through
their personal things. How did this happen I thought? Why didn't
they appreciate what we spent all day doing. I thought it looked
great and we would be rewarded for it. Well, at least thanked for
it. So we walked slowly back to Uncle Ricky's and was afraid to tell
him that we go into trouble. Well, Uncle Ricky wasn't angry at all,
well at least not with us. He told us that we did a good thing, but
how Tammy's parents could have taken offense to what we did
and how it wasn't good to be in someone's house who we didn't
know and didn't know us. He explained that we could have gotten

hurt or blamed if something turned up missing. We watched as my
Uncle Ricky walk over to their apartment and to what I thought
going to be an apology turned out that my Uncle Ricky wound
up telling them off. He stood up for us and said that they should
have been ashamed to have such a filthy apartment where it made
children want to clean it up! He came home and we went on with
our evening and Uncle Ricky told us that we did noting wrong. The
next day we didn't see Tammy or her brother at the pool, heck we
didn't see them the rest of our visit except from the window of
their apartment. Summer was almost over and we would go back to
Pittsburgh. I was glad to see mommy and it was good to back in our
own room. I always enjoyed travel but our home was always good
to come back too. My mother always knew how to make a house
a home. We always had coordinated sheets and wall paper, usually
more beautiful house than our peers. I didn't see that then too busy
just being a kid. I was happy about starting school that year it was
because I could now start practicing with the marching band.

My mother and Walter seemed to be in a groove, they made
our lives more balanced. They seemed to have it all and in my 4th
grade year they would get married. I now knew what took so long
for them, they each had to get divorced from their ex spouses.
They got married in front of the fire place in our very own living
room. Not a lot of guest mostly family. A few of Walters brothers
and their wives, his mom and her husband Carl (we called him
Uncle Carl) my grand mother Helen and my mother two siblings
and my Aunt Lois Buchanan. It was a nice ceremony and I mostly
remember the cake. It was light blue and white with sugar creme
icing. Funniest thing my baby sister asked if she could take a piece
of it to school for her teacher, so she did. It wasn't popular at those
times for children parents not to have been married before having
babies. She didn't know any better she was only in kinder garden.
Her teacher was glad to know that we were celebrating their union
and Holly was happy that her parents were now married, heck we
all were. Spring rolled around once more and I was getting excited

for my first parade. My mother took the whole day Friday to do our hair and polished the pre-owned marching boots, we were always buying uniforms of some sort, and that was the economical thing for her to do. I was involved in so many activities I don't know how my mother kept up. I was good at everything so she couldn't bring herself to let me know that my activities were costing her too much. So she spoke with my dance instructor and explained to her that she was taking both Lisa and I out. She was very understanding but offered my mother free tuition to keep me there. My mother told her that it wouldn't be right to choose me over Lisa, but my dance instructor explained to her that I was a natural and could go far and that Lisa wasn't that much into it as I was. Later Lisa would tell me that she could take it or leave it. I was so mad because if my mother knew that I'd might have been able to stay. I did keep up my other activities, not that they were free there were other cost like uniforms but we mostly had fundraisers of some sort in order to raise money for our travels. Some of the funding came from the school district. I also remained a cheerleader.

Middle School, utt ohh! There was only one middle school in our district that meant all of the children from all of the elementary schools came together. I think it was about 4 in total. There was Turner, Johnston, Kelly, and Simple. Other students made jokes about the children who attended Simple School. No need to put it in print, one could imagine. I didn't have an understanding for clicks at that time and boy were there many! I didn't belong to any of them. Much like the marching band I marched to my own drummer. It was a shock to me I had never seen girls who were so developed before. Lisa and I looked as if we were still in elementary school opposed to most of them. We had to take swimming at school and by that time I was a very strong swimmer and didn't have a need for it, but it was a requirement and I couldn't get out of it. As for me it was an easy A. Everything was easy for me at that time except for making friends. I didn't have a need for them I had Lisa and with all of my activities and homework there wasn't much time for anything else. Those years we very hard for us! We were popular because of our activities, however, not liked because of them. I couldn't understand why at the time. I hadn't developed anything that would make boys like me. I was so skinny and couldn't keep weight on for nothing in the world because of being so active. We didn't sit around all day playing video games there weren't any. No malls in our area with an arcade as of yet! Most of the kids weren't involved like us, they came from different back grounds and this was the generation when mom's started to work outside the home and were tired, which would explain why most of our friends weren't involved in after school activities. Our mother worked too, but somehow she still managed to keep up with the pace. We didn't know it either at the time that we were not rich because we never and I do mean never went without! We never had a utility off or no food in the house and we always traveled. We always were able to buy our uniforms and purchased school pictures, and travelled. Some children were on subsidy programs which we knew nothing of the sort. I remember my first encounter with a bully named Marlene. She was frightening to me for various reasons. One she was much more developed and much larger than I was and she wore a short afro that was no longer than one forth of an inch long. She was so tough even some of the boys tried not to get on her bad side. She bullied everyone except the people who she was friends with. She was much bigger than the average girl in my grade and much more developed much like a woman! I didn't think of her as attractive and she was mean as HELL. Looking back she probably was angry for some reasons we didn't know about. She lived in a big old house that needed care on the outside I couldn't imagine what it looked like on the inside. She had a lot of older brothers and sisters and wore the same cloths a lot. She hung out with a larger girl who lived across the street from her named Shawn. They were bully's! They made life unbearable for me in junior high. I would tell my mother about them and the others and she would tell me to kill them with kindness, I wasn't sure what she meant by that, but nothing seemed to stop them. One day in swimming class we were doing laps and my teacher was called out of the room for a minuet and Shawn and Marlene put a gym mat on top of me when I was coming up for air which pushed me back down into the water. Every time that I tried to get from underneath the mat they pushed it the direction of where I was swimming to. I was under water for quite some time and couldn't hold my breath any longer and was panic to say the least. Right before I was going to pass out my teacher came back into the room and saw that I was drowning. He pulled me out and gave me mouth to mouth. He knew that something went on and I was too afraid to tell him and hoped that they would stop bullying me since I didn't tell on them…fat chance those girls were mean to the core!

Then there was another mean girl nick named "Pig" I couldn't understand why anyone would name a cute girl like her such a funny nick name. When I think of a pig I think of a fat animal who is dirty and she was nothing of the sort. She was actually very cute and fashionable. I met her through my sister Lisa and I guess Lisa's mauto was keep your friends close and your enemies closer. Well, that didn't work either. We would both be told what to do and bullied around from Pig almost everyday. She made us walk her way home and then go home, which made our walk home take much longer. One day she made us come in her house after school, which was filthy, even more than Tammy's house in New Jersey (that we got in trouble for cleaning). Lisa seemed to like Pig in some odd way but I didn't. I never liked people who were bullies and who didn't follow rules. I believe that was a turning point for Lisa she was changing and becoming a bully herself! It was the 70's and mini skirts were fashionable and boys were now noticing girls and I forgotten that Lisa had scars. I was used to seeing them when we took baths, but she lived with it daily. Pig had older siblings too. Most families did back then. She had an older brother named Gerald. He was in 9th grade and at the high school right next door to our middle school. Well, Pig wanted me to go with her brother and I wasn't having it at all. I didn't like boys yet and heck he was in high school much to old for me...what was she thinking? Another day of walking Pig her way home from school. When we got close to her house I notice that her older brother and sister standing on their steps as if they were waiting for us. A gang of kids not many who I recognized were walking behind us as if they knew something that we didn't. Well, Pig's brother Gerald came running down those steps and before I knew what happened he swung a police bully club and hit me in the eye. I had never in my life felt such pain before. It was so hard that it felt like someone hit me from the back of my head. When I realized that we were being jumped by her family that was why the crowd had gathered around. My big brother Stanley came from out of no where and snatched a base ball bat from one of the on looking kids and commenced to kicking ass! He beat up Pig's big sister and Gerald. He didn't care if it was a girl or a boy all he saw was I was hurt. My mother was livid when we got home. She was sick of all the bulling. She never before that time told us that she too was bullied like that growing up. Remember when I said earlier about patterns. This one was from generation to generation, which made me think something was up?! My eye was very bad, it was closed up shut. It looked like a purple colored base ball with stretched skin over it. I was in pain for a very long time. It stayed like that for 6 months. I had to return to school like that the very next day. I was teased about it for weeks. Kids can be very cruel! I made a vial to myself that if I ever had children I would do what ever it took to keep them safe from all harm. The next day we walked home from school our usual way and Pig gather up a crowd to follow us home. My mother had to work that day but we knew Walter was home. We saw a crowd form and the closer we got to our house it was getting larger to where they were taking up not only our front yard but most of the street. Lisa and I ran in the house and got Walter. He went to front door and looked out and immediately called my mothers job. She was on her way home and he called the police. You could see fear in his eyes for us and couldn't imagine that this is what we were dealing with as kids. The police dispersed them like some sort of riot, it was a riot! This was ridiculous. There was absolutely no excuse for this sort of behavior and where in the hell were these peoples parents? That was the end of our days in Wilkinsburg. My mother purchased another house before we even sold that one on Clark Street. There were many more fights and bulling that I experienced there in Wilkinsburg, too many to name, and more to come at my new school in Penn Hills. We seemed not be able to escape it, but the only difference is that I learned to fight and fight I did! I didn't know that girls were jealous. Jealous because of what we did and had. Which is completely stupid. Children cannot help what their parents afforded them, or even be in control of what they look like. None of us can. I didn't join any activity to make anyone feel any sort of way.

I just like to do those sort of things and the truth about it I was extremely talented it just came naturally. I was so nieve I didn't even know that I was attractive.

I would find that out very shortly. With all of the commotion at Wilkinsburgh we moved in the middle of my 7th grade year. What a way to start, school was tough enough let alone to start in the middle of a school year. I really didn't care at that point I just wanted out of there. When I arrived a Penn Jr I had a teacher quickly show me around and then threw me in the mix. I remember walking down the hallway facing a group of African American boys walking towards me. Even though the school was set up differently than the one before. The hallways were wider but full of children. I thought I'd have an easier time since there were less black children and a better neighborhood…fat chance! Bullies come in every walk of life.

Well, this group of boys were mostly football players and other jocks. I didn't know about clicks however, unlike Wilkinsburgh I was going to become a fast learner of those things. The group of boys were Chuck, Ricky, Dennis and Russell. They looked like your average Junior High boys. Nothing special until you got to know them. Russell was a-lot like me very active and good at a lot of sports, Chuck was bigger than the rest of them and seemed to be the one with the biggest mouth...a prankster of sorts and class clown. Dennis seemed to be a follower at my initial assessment but none the lest. He and Ricky both ran track and were on the wrestling team. I notice a group of African American girls coming up behind them, one was named Niecy she was Penn Jr's only black cheerleader and girlfriend of Russell Boston which seemed to be against his wishes. She was not just a bully but bullied him into being her boyfriend as well. She kind of talked like "Oprah" when she played Harpo's wife in the movie "The Color Purple" very rough as if she wanted to fight all the time. On the side of her was Glenda, I don't think that they were friends just happened to be in the same spot at that time and then I got a taste of Chucks big mouth he said...hey Glenda we now got someone new prettier than you at our school. Well, thanks a lot. I seemed to have that nitched of making my own enemies. I didn't need his help. I didn't like him for that very reason. It took Glenda until we were grown to see I wasn't her enemy. Niecy didn't care or think much of me as long as no one messed with her boyfriend Russell. I didn't care he too wasn't my type, especially since he wasn't strong enough to shake Niecy off. Dennis was easy going and a good friend to Ricky. Ricky would become one of my closest friends later when I finally discovered boys. Niecy kept her eyes on me and Russell she was so controlling for such a young girl. What I didn't know at the time is when people who are intimate without the institution of marriage, they become insecure with the relationship because they don't have ownership or the legal right to that person. She didn't have to worry about me with that, I wasn't into boys as of yet. However, I would take something else from her...her spot on the cheerleading squad. I didn't know about racism at the time. I only had one other experience when we lived in Wilkinsburg I was in the forth grade. I went home after school with a friend from my class named Jill. She was blonde and was my best friend. When Jill's father came home from work and looked outside and saw me in their pool with his daughter swimming he yelled…What is that Nigger doing in my pool! I didn't know what that word meant but I knew that it was bad and it was directed at me because the only person in the pool was his daughter Jill. His wife was so embarrassed and before she could offer me a ride home I jumped out of the pool and ran all the way home without putting on my clothes. By the time I got home I was dried off. Getting back to Penn Jr. It was mostly white. You were lucky should you have another black student in your class. The classes were large and the school was predominantly made up of very large Italian families. I didn't know that they would only choose one African American girl to be on the squad. It was made up of at least 14 girls so why just one black? I didn't care who would be the looser to that odd, I just knew it wasn't going to be me. Sure enough…I won and Niecy was mad as HELL! Fighting mad! She was so concerned about loosing Russell to a girl she never thought about loosing her spot on the cheerleading squad to any one. That was the beginning of a very bad relationship for us and the beginning for me to have more haters. They were no longer my bullies, they became my haters because I learned to fight! I wasn't going to except the bulling any more, and no one was going to ever stop me from getting what I wanted out of life and doing what I wanted to do…and I mean NO ONE!!! There were a few more fights along the way. One so terrible Niecy's sister bit my sister Lisa in the face. It was cheered on by one of my mothers haters. Patterns…Generational…you see. Kanya West said it best in one of his songs, hater nigga's marry hater bitches and have hater kids, so true. When you become conscious of it no matter what side of it you are on you can break free of it, it's called generational curses. Jealously is a demonic spirit and can be broken. I wasn't yet aware of it and I was going to beak mine but not before it made me a fighter. I was so tired of being bullied that some time

I fought the wrong people I just didn't care any more, I just wanted it to stop at any cost! Every year I made the squad except one year and it was because of an injury I got during my freshmen year. My friend Vedora filled the one spot that year, saved for a girl of color. She later told me she knew as soon as I healed, that I was coming back for my spot and I did exactly that. So that year I just mostly worked after school. I for an African American dentist named Dr. James Wilson. He had his own practice that he ran along with his wife and they had two small toddlers. I started out baby sitting for them after school and some times on the weekends when they would have date night. I enjoyed being busy and not at home my sisters would keep stuff going. Lisa was bossy and Holly was spoiled and a little insecure because she hadn't come into her own yet. It was rough being the middle sister and I wanted peace some where and wouldn't stay any place long enough for some sort of fight to break out. So I mostly stayed in a structured environment. It was my safety net. By the time my senior year came around I was so ready to get the heck out of Pittsburgh. I did get out but mostly in the summers when we would go to New York to visit my father as we did every summer and sometimes we'd go over to New Jersey and stay with my step fathers people. My Uncles were very kind to us they treated us as of we were their very own. I enjoyed every one of those visits with them. They were mature for their age and very responsible. On the other had I grew tired of visiting my father I loved him very much and knew that he loved me. He was so depressed and became a heavy drinker and always asked me about my mother and say that she still was his wife, even though it was clear that she had moved on and I felt very sorry that he could. He just slipped into a depression that he needed God and only God to get him out. I do believe in professional help, however, I mainly put my trust in God. Don't get me wrong there are some good people who are out here, however the Bible says trust in no man. People are human and make mistakes and some of those mistakes may take you the rest of your life trying to get over or through.

The summer right before my senior year of high school. I finally got a boyfriend his name was Tony Vennie. I know his name sounds Italian but he wasn't. He was a year younger than I was, however, he was more my speed. He was cute and played football and came from one of the sweetest families. He was the youngest of three and I fit right in the family. Our love for one another reminded me something of an "after school special" pure and sweet. However, somewhere the summer between my Jr and Sr year I would loose my virginity with Tony. We discussed it with his parents and not mine. By this time mom and Walter had separated and she was having a rough time with it. She loved him and so did other women and a few men. Walter was FINE! Not my type I like dark men but Walter was the exception to everyones rule. It really wasn't Walters fault, women pushed themselves on him so much that he had to literally run from them. I saw it a few times for myself. What was he supposed to do, even my mothers sister wanted him. Nevertheless my mother was broken hearted for a minuet and wasn't paying close attention to her children anymore. Heck we didn't need her much either we were growing up. Tony's family supported me and went to almost every game so I had a ride home with them. That was probably their way of making sure I didn't get pregnant. Getting pregnant wasn't in any future plans for me, I was going to travel and do something great I thought… who had time for marriage and children. Thank goodness that I had those type of dreams because Tony and I didn't last not even to the end of the year. However he did give me a friendship ring for Christmas in front of his entire family including his grand mother. I was so embarrassed. His parents thought we were too serious but it was Tony, then after he cheated with Glenda, that was my excuse to be done. I knew I had plans for frying much bigger fish or so I thought. As long as Michael Jackson was single I kept my options open…lol. One good thing that I did like about myself I never wanted revenge I just simply moved on and was excited about the next thing. My senior year my mother needed a break and was stressed from her separation from Walter. So she gave her play cousin that she grew up with (who was married to "Stevie Wonder"). Her name was Syreeta Wright and for many years I never knew that we weren't biologically related. Our Buchanan Family and Syreeta's parents and grand parents were so intertwined, it wasn't until I was in my late 30's before I learned the truth. When my mother returned from her visit with Syreeta, she looked wonderful. Syreeta took her every where and treated her to every spa treatment known to man kind at that time. Syretta lived in Ladera Heights (rather known as the Black Beverly Hills). She too was divorced from Stevie by this time but still was in the music business. She wrote most of his earlier greatest hits for him like "Signed Sealed Delivered" and "You are the Sunshine of my Life" she even sang on them. When I saw how good my mother looked when she returned I couldn't wait to get my hands on a ticket out of Pittsburgh! That was the plan…

About a month later in January 1982 I learned about a pageant for young black girls. It was ran by a woman named Jean Bryant and she was from New Jersey. I don't know her back story in how she came to Pittsburgh but she wasn't anything like the women here. She was running things and making a name for herself and full of class. Strong intelligent and a producer her own thing. I liked that! Well, I got signed right up and was front and center for the first rehearsal. By this time I was already over Tony and had a new focus…winning this pageant. I knew what I would do for the talent part, I could dance my butt off and by that time I was confident in the way I looked or at least excepted the way I looked. I thought I was too skinny, that was all I heard in school or when a boy couldn't date me they would say that's all right I never wanted her any ways she is too skinny. When I would later move to "Hollywood" I would find out that skinny wasn't a bad thing actually it was an asset!

We had practice for the "Miss Black Teenage Pageant" every Saturday mornings, up until Mother's Day in May there went any free time. I was now cheering for the varsity basketball team and working for Dr. Wilson still but now as a Dental Assistant. He put up with all of my activities. I only remember one time of him getting on me for being late. I tried my very best not to disappoint him. I heard his wife complain a few times I sometimes thought she didn't like me. He knew I was going places in life and believed and supported me in every way. He made me believe that I could do anything even become a Dentist or even have my own business one day like him. Maybe he was the reason that I admired older dark complected self made men, the subconscious is a mess. I enjoyed practice I could hear my mothers voice in my head…that practice makes perfect! I had only one problem, my mother hadn't yet signed me in. She was working nights and Saturday mornings was her only rest period. Every Saturday I would stand over her bed and beg her to go with me. I told her that they threatened to throw me out if I showed up another time without her signing me in and that was the truth. Well, I caught the bus one more time anyhow without her and when I got down town Pittsburgh to the location and at break time Ms. Bryant pulled me a side and scolded me for not bringing my mother I explained why, she immediately took me in her private office and dialed my mother I was afraid that my mother would be asleep and answer the phone in a nasty tone and she did, but as soon as she heard it was Ms. Bryant she straightened up. Ms. Bryant had a very authoritative way about herself. I was glad that she called my mother so my mother would know that I told her the truth and that if she didn't show up that I would be kicked out. Ms. Bryant told her something that she probably didn't mean to say in front of me…she said Ms. Clark you really should come to see your daughter at practice she has a real possibility of winning this pageant! Well, that was all my mother needed to hear, she had her butt down there front and center the following week.

My mother came with me the following week to practice. She was so proud. When we got home she spoke with a few of her friends on the phone and I could hear her brag about how good I was and what Ms. Bryant told her and that I was a really good dancer and how she'd put me in dance classes since I was very young and on and on. I was happy that she wasn't angry about having missed her Saturday morning sleep.

Our basket ball team had made it to the finals and I still had the pageant practices and still working for Dr. Wilson, but not that much anymore. I was so busy that I hadn't remembered that I hadn't lined up a prom date yet and it was getting late in the game. I couldn't take Ricky he already had a date and I had him escort me when I was on "Home Coming Court" and again I was the only black girl who was selected for that position or honor. I was still Tony's girlfriend at that time but he was on the football team and opt to play in the game which was kind of dumb...he was a junior and could have played following year. He could have used that time to "Shine" with me. I bet his senior year he wasn't dating anyone on the "Home Coming Court". Youth is waisted on the young! Our basketball finals were in the home stretch. We were playing Peabody High School at Peabody. My sister Lisa was at the game not for me or even to watch. She only went to that game because Peabody was known for having all the cute guys. She and her girlfriends were only there to mack! She kept trying to talk to me at the game and I was getting annoyed with her. I had to be focused and watch for which cheer we would do from the side lines or which cheer we would do at timeout. They were playing for the playoff and it was down to the wire. Finally the game was over and of course we won. Penn Hills was undefeated in the 1980's in all forms if sports. We were one of few high schools who had Archery, Riffle Team and Golf. We had a very big budget and competitive students of all kinds. Most of the guys in my class and the year before went on to play professional football. Lisa came over to me after the game and she was walking with a boy I thought she was going to introduce me to him as someone she'd just met. Instead she said in her very bold way of talking..."Debbie meet Brian he just agreed to take you to the prom". I was so embarrassed but not for long Brian was cute and had the most beautiful green eyes not too tall but not short. He was a solid young man well traveled and educated. He didn't attend either school and that started off our conversation. I asked him why was he there since he didn't attend either school. He told me that he lived near by in one of Pittsburgh most affluent neighborhoods (ShadySide). He was new to the city and attended Alderdice High School. We hit it off right away and exchanged numbers I wasn't mad a Lisa as we walked out of the gymnasium. She said to me…"now you have a prom date little sister" as if it were just that simple.

Brian was as excited for meeting me as well. A prom date shouldn't have been a problem for him. He was good looking charming and came fro great stock! His father was the Attorney General of Guam and his mother was the first African American female Assistant D.A here in Pittsburgh. The problem wasn't Brian getting a prom date, it was him getting a date that would past the test of his mother Trudy! He called me as soon as we both got home that night and we talked for a very long time. Since the next day was Sunday he brought his mother over to meet my mom. Thank goodness Brian was a take charge kind of dude or things might not have taken place. He knew that we were pressed for time and since I had the pageant coming up my schedule was pretty tight.

Besides I hadn't past the Trudy test yet. He needed time just incase I didn't pass Trudy's expectations. Somehow this didn't bother me. I was very competitive and was used to being judged in various things. What could she not like about me I thought. I was reasonably cute, great student and very active in school and heck I even had a job working for a Doctor (not your everyday high schooler's employment). Even now I had the possibility of being a pageant winner.

I told my mother that they were coming over and how I met him and that it was Lisa's idea in the first place, she didn't seem to mind she had her rest and my mother was a people person especially after she had her rest. She'd always made a big diner on Sundays so she wouldn't be going out of her way. Here comes Brian and Trudy, she was a breath of fresh air. She was full of life, class, frisky and a whole lot of fun! She instantly loved me and she was extremely impressed with my family history. She knew what it was like to study Law and raise children on her own (now that Trudy and her ex-husband were divorcing). She looked at me and Brian as the next generation power couple and she instantly had plans for the two of us. I could still see the wheels turning inside her head. I didn't know that Brian had already been excepted to "Duke University" in Durham, NC. It was enough to find me a prom dress and costume for the pageant…OMGoodness, I had forgotten that I hadn't completed my college applications. I knew that I had a fall back and attend Alabama A&M since my great great grand father Rev. Dr. William Hooper Councill Esq. was the founder and my other great grand father Dr. Walter Solomon Buchanan was the first president there as well. But I didn't know if I wanted to go that far away from home and I was tired of being the first in everything. People who are the first are the ones who take the biggest risk and hits. No one in the history of my family has ever attended since we migrated here to Pittsburgh (strange), and I wasn't sure if I wanted that challenge. Well, Trudy got busy and told me to meet her down town one day this coming week after school at Saks Fifth Ave she wanted to help style me for prom. Well, my mother didn't want her to go out of her way but what my mother didn't know that Trudy was the type of person who wasn't going to go out her way if she didn't feel like doing something…she wanted to do this and so I allowed her. We enjoyed ourselves the Sunday Trudy and Brian came by. It was a chance for me and Brian to get to know one another we only had a few weeks. You would have thought we were planning our wedding day or something how fast things were moving. When I met with Trudy that coming week, she was dressed in a navy blue suit looking professional and powerful as most women did down town Pittsburgh. She look as if she should be working at the "White House" or something! That's why Brian wasn't intimidated by me, I was like his mother a "Go Getter"! We went to the fine dress department and I believe that it was the first

time that I had ventured inside Saks Fifth Ave. I wasn't intimidated
in fact I felt right at home. They brought her a glass of wine and
Trudy was ordering them around as if I were Royalty! In fact I
was. Scottish Royalty. My great grand father Dr. Walter Solomon
Buchanan Sr. is from along that line. I would later get documents
from Carnegie Mellon University from one of the Historians. My
mothers father Walter Solomon Buchanan Jr. would tell me of
our history when he came to visit and kept us up late night with
his drinking. He told us about his days on the road with my step
grand mother "Dinah Washington" and all of the Jazz Greats he'd
worked with and his recordings. Trudy purchased my dress it was
a light teal taffeta off the shoulders ball gown. I was very much
satisfied but I was concerned about her spending so much money
on my dress because she just met me. To make me feel better about
the cost of the gown Trudy told me to wear it for the pageant, so
I may get additional wear out of it which made me feel a lot better
about the price. Now I only needed to find a costume for my talent.
Later that week I did. I found a beautiful red one shouldered dress
made of the same fabric (taffeta). It was right below my knee and
I told Trudy about it and she gave me her credit card to purchase
it. I didn't tell my mom Trudy wanted to do it. She knew having
3 daughters was expensive for any parent, especially being how
active I was. Besides my mother paid for all of the other things like
hair, nails and under garments things of that sort which added up
very fast. Also my mother hired a professional choreographer to
choreograph my performance when she received that little piece of
information from Ms. Bryant that I could possibly win. My school
made an announcement over the PA system that I and a few other
girls would be in the pageant this coming Sunday on Mother's Day.
Most of us from the black community knew any how that was a big
event for us. It was now time for the Big Event! Show and prove.
I wasn't nervous at all. I was accustom to pro-forming in front
of people. Heck most of the girls would be the top of their game
at in their schools. Only very few did this pageant on a whelm.
Looking back Ms. Bryant was so professional, back stage was just

like a "Miss America" pageant. No chaos and for most of the part
no tears or at least not yet. Most of my family were here to see me.
All of my siblings my mother Aunt Juanita from New York (which
really was my fathers ex girlfriend who took care of us during
our visits with him) Brian and Trudy. What I didn't know that my
future husband would be there and said something to me after it
was over and when we were later married he brought it up which
let me know just how sneaky he was. Why didn't he tell me sooner
like when we started dating. I was enjoying the event so much that I
forgot we were competing against one another. Whenever we were
lined up in the back we got to see portions of the others girls talent
segment. There was also a period when were all on stage together
when we walked out individually said our names, where we were
from, our age and what school we attended. Then we took our bow
all together. The pageant was very long and after they announced
the fifteen finalist, those were the girls who got to preform their
talents live then brought us all back to announce the final 3 and
the crown the winner. I didn't think nothing of it until they called
the final 3… OMGoodness, I was in the top three. That was
when I first thought I could actually win. Everyones families were
screaming their heads off. It sound like we were at a "Steeler" game
headed towards the "Super Bowl"! Then came the questioning by
the judges…I can't tell you who went first I just know I was some
where in-between. I will never forget my question because it was
so simple and very broad…"if I had one wish what would it be"?
Well, heck, I thought to win this pageant for my mother as a gift to
her since it was Mother's Day, but then I thought no that would be
selfish so I answered… for World Peace. Heck we weren't at war at
time, what in the heck was I thinking…when it came to Sharon, I
don't remember what exactly what her question was but she was a
real church going girl and she gave a sermon on the mountain and
finished up with… "and with God on my side"…and that was all
she wrote…Sharon was crowned! I will admit that girl could sing!

One down two to go. Brian's prom came before mine and I didn't want to wear my dress 3 times in a row. So I wore a hot pink chiffon dress similar to but not as nice as the one Trudy got me. It was at the William Penn Hotel down town Pittsburgh a very exclusive hotel. When Brian and I got off the elevator the first thing I saw was my dress on another girl. Well, that wasn't going to happen to me and I made Brian take me home to change. Trudy found that so funny she loved that I would do something like that because that would be something she'd do. When we returned after I changed we had missed the diner portion of the prom. Brian could put up with my antics because he was cut from the same cloth. I was still trying to figure out what to do after High School, everyone had received their acceptance letters to what University's they would attend. Most were attending local state schools which I wanted no part of. I didn't want to go too far away from home. As a matter of fact I hadn't thought much of where because deep down I knew that my mother wouldn't agree with my dream of doing hair and design. I was very creative and enjoyed all things creative. I loved to style people and give them make overs. Even when I got my own place I was even great at home decorating even when I hardly had money, I could do things on a budget, but how would I tell her, would she understand? And Trudy, she had big hopes for me too. Most of them probably included me as her daughter in-law. I wasn't ready for all of this ...wish I could buy some time. I never knew that I could ask God for direction, I was never taught that. We went to church based on respect for God but not having real under standing of His role in our lives. And if God was talking to me how could I hear His voice? So after my prom was over and summer was here I still hadn't decided and Trudy had an idea that would keep me close to Brian. She asked my mother if I could go with them for the summer for a bit of a road trip. Of course I wanted to go. Right after promI had got into a fight with my brother and he blacked my eye (more patterns) seems as if someone doesn't want me to see or to speak. One of my trips to visit my father in between 8th and 9th grade my cousin Russell pushed me off of a mail box and chipped my front teeth real bad, that was how I met Dr. Willson. I am paying more close attention to names and words as I am writing. You see, in the beginning was the Word…God spoke words into existence, therefore words have power, words must be very important to God. We can build someone up by our words or we can kill with our words. I was a cheerleader and naturally build people up with my words! But who was going to do that for me. All people seemed to do was fight me.

So off I went with Trudy, Brian and Trudy's boyfriend whom she knew from Washington D.C, and that's where we were headed to. She would take us on a tour to see the "White House" the "Monument" and every attraction DC had to see. I was still sad and Trudy gave me a pair of her designer sunglasses to wear on account of my black eye. Brian comforted me as best as he could and offered to fight my brother I told him no on account Stanley was bigger and stronger and a bit hostile since he'd been in the military. Trudy's boyfriend had the typical BrownStone row house in DC, something out of a movie scene. It was really nice and comfortable. Warm is a better word. He was a scholar and had a lot of law books, actually there were books every where. Trudy put me and Brian in the same room to sleep in…that was different for a mother I thought. She knew that I was very upset about my black eye and knew we'd probably wouldn't mess around which she was right. I was embarrassed that my own family behaved like we didn't love or respect one another, and we didn't. I didn't care what I was going to do about school, I made up my mind that I was going to get out. We stayed there a few more days. We dined at fancy restaurants and Trudy treated us like adults. That's probably why Brian was so cultured. Well, the next morning we put our things in the car and got on the road. The next stop "Duke University". That would be the first time I was on an Ivy League campus. It was intimidating for me only because I knew that I couldn't afford something like that. I didn't feel out of place mostly because that was what my family was all about "Higher Education". I just didn't desire it for myself and thought that they wouldn't understand. How could I not want this and my great great grand father worked tirelessly to obtain his own University to make our lives better not just for us but for all people of color. Which left me confused to why I was treated badly by my own people. Didn't they know I was for them…my family was for them.

We would take a tour of the campus and show Brian which dorm he'd be staying in. It looked to me like a bunch of rich white entitled kids who's parents had their lives mapped out. They didn't notice me or my black eye. After we left Duke and Brian had to return right back for some STP program. Can't remember what that stood for, I was just trying to figure out what was I going to do in the mean time.

Next we headed to the beach. Trudy was like medicine for the sick. She knew that I needed peace and a gentle push in the right direction. She was thinking what she thought was the best thing for me, Brian and herself. While we were at the beach she told me that there was a more affordable school in the same vicinity as Duke, then me and Brian could be there for one another and would I like to check it out, so I agreed. On the way back we stopped a North Carolina Central University in Durham. It was a much smaller University an HBCU like my great great grandfathers. Very well kept. Trudy immediately went to the registrar's office to see if they had any scholarships and in what area. I don't know if she told them who's grand daughter I was but she had a way with people and Trudy mostly got what she wanted. They told her that there was an opening for a "Special Talent" scholarship and they asked what talent did I have. Well, Trudy told them that I just placed in a local pageant back in Pittsburgh and one thing Southerns love is a pageant girl! She told them how great I performed and that she attended the pageant herself. The University had a dance company and I could audition for it and should I get the scholarship, I could work there to make up the difference for my tuition. One thing about me I was never a shy person and I enjoyed dancing. Sound like a good plan except it wasn't my plan. Everyone had ideas for my life and I just didn't have any, I knew what I wanted to do I just didn't have a clue about how to obtain it, or brave enough to live my own dreams.

CHAPTER FIVE

If any one wanted to know what my college experience was like I tell them to watch the movie "School Daze" by Spike Lee. He must have attended an HBCU. Brian was settled in and couldn't meet me at the bus station. I left Pittsburgh on Continental Trailways Bus. It took a long 11 hours with $200.00 dollars to my name and a trunk with all of my things, oh yeah and a bit of HOPE. I called the University and they sent someone over to pick me up and then we learned that the housing office forgot to set me up with a dorm. So I stayed a day with the woman who picked me up from the bus station. She only seemed to accomodate me out of duty. I keep waiting for her Southern Hospitality to kick in. I knew the difference in the way I was raised and especially since Trudy had been so warm and loving since the time we met. Trudy was a very busy woman and never made me feel any thing but special, even when she only had a minuet for me. She was present. I never felt quite welcomed in the South, including my great great grand fathers town that he founded and University. I'm not sure if they are just Clannish or suspicious maybe a little of both, or maybe they haven't gotten over the "Cvil War", but these were my own people...I don't know what I expected? I wasn't received well in my own home town either, and not to compare myself with Jesus, but He wasn't excepted either. So what was I supposed to learn from this and what would be my major...

Brian couldn't wait to get across town and get to my campus. He was a sight for sore eyes, but looked terribly out of place. He was a collegian kid and everyone on my campus knew he didn't belong and neither I at Duke. I was metropolitan and most could tell that I wasn't from those parts. However, he would come by as much as possible. Once classes started sometimes Brian and I wouldn't talk for a 2 week period. I would imagine his courses were much more challenging than mine and I was struggling for the first time academically. I met a few people and some of the girls were nice but that is how they were raised to be hospitable and genteelly, I just call it phony. Sometimes I wondered if they just really wanted express their true feelings. And sometimes they did, just with a smile on their face. I could see right through them, even with all the black eyes that I had..it didn't take natural eyes to see that, I was developing my inner man.

Homecoming came around and my cousin Blain was attending one of the local state school in Pittsburgh. He contacted me and some of my friends from Pittsburgh who were in college. I wondered how did they find me…heck I didn't know where I was going until just a few months ago. They all heard I was attending an HBCU and we had the best parties. We did have great parties, Brian might have disagreed since he was at Duke, I beg to differ, all they seemed to do was get drunk. After their parties the campus would smell of vomit and stale beer. I could tell Brian wasn't happy either and his grades were about as bad as mine, but my options were running out fast and so I decided to give this my best shot. I was glad to see my cousin when he came to visit me during Home Coming. It is a big to do at HBCU's. He couldn't wait for me to introduce him to some southern bells. I told him that I didn't have close friends back home what made him think that things would be any different here. I just changed locations not my views or personality. But that could have been the problem…and since I had changed locations, why hadn't I tried to change my views? But a few of the guys had their eyes one me, but I wasn't to sure about them either. I spent my summers in Harlem and those were the type of guys that I was attracted to. Street savvy authentic men who marched to their own drum not frat boys who appeared to have a need to feel powerful when part of a group. Later when I married I got to witness the charitable work that some of them did. However, one can do those things on your own. My fore fathers belonged to some social organizations, however, they were too busy starting businesses, schools, earning degrees and the next big thing. I liked that about my father as well. He was his own man. My cousin Blain and I went to the Q party. It was dark and in some sort of basement. Purple lights (which is one of their colors) much like a gang…not too much different, same concept. (a group of people who worked together in order to achieve a goal), some time excluding others is what I didn't care for. The music was good, party music like "Trouble Funk" and "Rair Essence" rump shakin music. We danced and one of the guys gave me a cup of "Purple Passion" it's made of grape kool aid and grain alcohol…deadly. I wasn't a drinker or a person who like to test my limits, the only reason that I did was because my cousin was there and he would cover me, or so I thought. The next thing I knew I was in the bathroom with a line outside wanting to know who was in there taking so long. Well, the purple passion was a rotten fruit and needed to come out and it did. The next thing I knew a guy came in there and helped me up off the floor in front of the bowl. His name was Victor and a Q who played football (again see the patterns). He played the gentleman at first and even let my cousin stay in the male dorm room with him. It was a set up I thought to gain my trust. Later he would show his true colors. I never really cared for him, just somebody that I met along the way. Blain had a good time and had to get back to school himself.

I finally heard from Brian and he wasn't too happy about being at Duke either and needed a shoulder to lean on. I needed one too, but neither of us knew how to be there for one another any more. We weren't quite mature enough to know what to do. This is why I believe a lot of college students don't do well their freshman year. I just thought that this was something all males knew by just being born male. I thought that it was just women who were needy. I later learned that it is all mankind. That is why so many people are searching for truth, trying everything to fill that void, until they get that void feed with something meaningful. It's a hunger that no one can fill but God! I still haven't discovered that at that point in my life, so I kept on searching. I was drawn down the street to Mt. Carmel Baptist Church. I went on a Sunday looking for something familiar. There were a few students there from my campus. I later joined and got Baptized. I was so proud of myself and even though I had no understanding of what I just did. I don't even remember if they gave me any classes before the actual ceremony and if they did I don't remember what they thought me. Any ways maybe I was feeling lonely and a little dirty and thought this would somehow wash my sins away.

I met two girls on my floor that I would sometimes hang with or we would together eat at the mess hall. Their names were Paulette and Tanya. They were both from Silver Springs, MD. I don't believe that they knew each other before they came to school here but got very close quickly being they pretty much seemed to have the same interest and background. Paulette was cool but was a little love sick being her boyfriend was attending school in Atlanta. Most of her free time was spent waiting in line for the only pay phone on our floor. No cell phones as of yet except for the really big ones you'd only see rich white business men with. She was either studying or searching for quarters to talk to her boyfriend named Champ. I never met him but I knew him through her. Tanya said she had someone too except I never saw her seeking him out or anyone contacting her.

After "Home Coming" my mother and her boyfriend Charlie would come to see me. They brought care packages and Charlie was good to slip you a little money for the road. They didn't stay long and I hadn't to much to show them besides the campus. I did tell my mother that I found a church she didn't seem to care as long as it would help me not to get pregnant while I was there that was all she seem to care about. As a matter of fact, that's what she asked me. I did gain my freshman 15, it was because of all that southern cooking. We had very good food, I would get up early to have breakfast even on cold days. Charlie gave me some money to purchase a plane ticket to come home for Thanksgiving (that would be the first time I flew on an airplane) and made me promise that I wouldn't use it for anything else.

I was supposed to come home for Christmas however, Paulette and Tanya invited me to stop over in DC along the way. They said that they had a lot of parties to attend and always bragged how great DC was. Even though I had just been to DC with Trudy and Brian, I wanted to experience it with girlfriends. I knew it would be a much different experience. Well, I would stay at Tanya's house. She had 3 siblings much like myself and raised by a single mom. Her mother was sweet but so tired she didn't even care that I was there for the weekend. My mother would have had a fit. She's the type who likes to prepare for guest. I know why our house was never dirty. We grew up with chores and my mother was a little OCD. Heck so were me and my sisters. We can organize our butts off. Tanya's house was a bit relaxed. I was ok until I spotted that her little dog did his business in the bed and she never freaked out. I knew where not to lay my head. I was surprised...no meal was made, nothing offered, I was starting to think this was a bad idea. Maybe I should have gone straight home to Pittsburgh. We decided to go out and I was glad. Maybe I could get something to eat then. So we packed ourselves into the bathroom to put on our makeup and style our hair. I was ok being crammed into a bathroom being that I had sisters. My mother always encouraged travel, mostly to see how other people live and how the world operates. I still believe it's one of the "BEST" forms of education. We were blessed to live as if had a two parent income household. Even when we didn't have both parents in the household simultaneously. After we got dressed and went out on a night of the town. I remember it was freezing. We went to a couple of parties, one in a modern apartment own by some guy Tanya knew. I kept listening in on everyones conversations hoping to hear something meaningful or with substance. I guess none of us had any. I just knew it wasn't for me...but what was? I always seem to not know what I didn't want but what was it that I desired?

So we all pilled up in Tanya's brother car and went to our next destination. He went to Central as well but was about to graduate. He had a baby at home in DC. That would be the first time I knew a guy with a baby out of wed lock. I was so green. While we were listening to the radio in the car we heard an announcement over the airwaves for Debra Clark please call home. How did my mother know that I would stop over in Washington DC, I will never know. I guess a mothers intuition. Boy they had jokes on me for months to come. I would get on the bus the next day and did not care even if I got a beating when I got home. I just wanted a hot home cooked meal, a bath and my very own bed with no dog mess in it.

When I got home to Pittsburgh, some of my old friends stopped by and I was glad to see them. Vedora was one of them she would always be the one to find me where ever I moved to. They all seemed to be enjoying college life but I couldn't bring myself to tell them the truth. I didn't like my major or my classes and to this day I can't name one professor except Ms. Pinckney my dance instructor. Ms. Pinckney seemed to be hard on me. Maybe because she might have thought I was being wasteful and squandering my scholarship but I wasn't. I was being the obedient child that I always was and listening to what everyone thought I should be doing. I wasn't listening to the voice of God in me to find my divine purpose. So I kept being obedient to the adults around me until I searched all over this earth for my purpose. However, I would return back to Central after the much needed break at home. It was reluctant, nevertheless I returned. I was so behind and not focused. Funny I cannot remember any professors reaching out to me like "child what are you doing"? But this was the difference between college and high school, you were on your own and it wasn't your professors job to encourage you.

I was dating a guy named Eric. He was sort of a playboy. The funny thing about southern men, just because they behaved like gentlemen on the outside, inside they sometimes had different motives. I could see right through them. What I liked about Harlem men is what you see is what you get. No pulling the wool over your eyes, just straight shooters. They don't cheat on you behind your back they tell you up front and give you the option. Well, Valentine's Day was coming and I wanted to see what if any thing he may do. He was a "Kappa" and they were having a "Sweet Hearts" dance. I didn't know that this wasn't anything new. I am not much big on tradition(except for my home and my taste in furniture). However I like to mix it up a bit. My style is more eclectic. I may share that same aspect in men. So Paulette and I would go together, I really wanted to see out of plain curiosity who Eric brought to the dance... if any. We were bored with nothing to do, since her man was in Atlanta, she went to be supportive of me. Actually Eric's fraternity brother road Paulette and I back to campus., except Paulette had to drive he was drunk by the end of the night and then hit on me. That was common practice of fraternity boys in college and I don't like anything typical. Like I said I always knew what I didn't want. I just couldn't figure out just how in the heck did I marry one later in life. I am currently reading a book now titled "The bait of Satan". It helps you to see him for who and what he is. When there are patterns in your life generally Satan is in the mix. Especially when the patterns aren't good. It's designed to keep you from moving forward in you life, or discovering your purpose from God. To keep you going in circles and not moving forward in life. And when you find God in a real way, thats when the process can start of getting set FREE, but you also have to put in the work. At that point on my journey I was still searching.

The school year would be over and my grade point average was good enough to return as a sophomore not so much for Brian. He dropped out of Duke and joined the Army. I know it broke Trudy's heart. Both of Brian's parents were Attorneys and expected much of him, but parent sometimes seeking so much education and forget to train up a child in the Way it should go. It's also a trap to think education is going to be the answer for every thing in life. Yes, it is good to have one, however, there are some things in life that you can't learn in a class room.

Once more I was glad to be home but each time I came home to visit things seemed different mainly because I was different. I was changing, not necessarily growing making large strides but nevertheless I was at least seeking. I got a summer job at Kaufmann's Department Store down town. Mostly modeling, it was fast money and you didn't at that time need an agency. I had one but I booked jobs myself all the time. They came to me. I had a Regal-ness about myself and confidence. When I would watch Tyra Banks modeling show, I would hear her and her staff comment on beauty. I agree with my mother that beauty is in the eye of the one beholding!

By this time there was no one in the house but mommy, Holly, (who was still in High School) and myself. Holly wasn't the A student however she would do well in College and complete her Masters Degree at the University of Maryland.

I wasn't home most of the time and my mother was certainly over Walter by now and she was dating and working. I was happy for her, that we all were almost out of the way and she could now begin to focus on herself. I met a guy named Jerry that summer (another Kappa) but he wasn't exactly a typical fraternity guy. I am sure he'd be glad to know that I viewed him this way. He had an independent life from them and didn't rely on what they could for him. He came from a close-knit family and they were from Philadelphia, which is probably why he was different from the guys here in Pittsburgh. His father was a Pastor of his own church and Jerry had lots of siblings. Even one of his sisters resembled me. Her name was Lisa like my sister. He and I would hang out for the summer nothing serious just having fun. He always had the best of things including his car. He drove a BMW and that was big time for someone his age. He even had his own photography studio down town. He wasn't frugal and didn't mind taking me places with him, I was good company. We both had outgoing personalities. I considered Jerry intelligent probably because his parents didn't skip Spiritual training. Now that doesn't mean that it would make Jerry a perfect guy, however any additional training anyone has is an asset to me. In the fall I would return back to Central but this time I wasn't sure just how long that I would last. I tried to hint around to my mother while I was there for the summer but I never came out with it. Her life seemed much more smooth and I didn't want to mess up her grove. I bumped into Eric when I got back to school. I could see his relationship with his girlfriend had taken a more serious turn. He tried not to let it show but it was apparent to me. I must say she was a knock out when I saw her and they looked good together they were both very tall and they both had sex appeal. I wasn't upset and I didn't need much of an excuse. It would be weeks before Eric even knew that I left college. I was surprised even to get the call, how gentlemen of him...

Oh Lord, I dropped out of school. I told my mother after my visit at Thanksgiving break 1983 that I would not be returning. I will never forget her face! She looked at me as if I were going to be another disappointment in her life. Since she couldn't undo her life she had put her hopes in mine. How does one live their life for others and please ones self...you can't.

I knew that I could not come home and be any sort of a bourdon to my mother. The first thing that she said to me if you are not in school you better have a job. That was a given, I didn't plan to come home and vegetate. I've had a job since I was 14 working for Dr. Wilson. I got one the very next day. Kaufmann's Department Store was glad to have me full time. I worked all over that store and modeled at all of the others as well. I was making money and burning the candle at every end I could find. With Trudy's introduction of Saks Fifth Ave, I got a taste for the finer things and was willing to work for them as well. Jerry and I would pick up right where we left off lunch dates evenings out in ShadySide listening to jazz but he wouldn't take me to meet his parents yet. What he didn't know that I already knew his father and sister Lisa from church. They were friends of my Pastor and we were regulars at each others church being both churches were COGIC

Going back to work at Kaufmann's Department Store was good for me. Even though today it no longer exists, it will always be an "Historic Landmark" in the city. It is still a meeting place for people. Everyone who's lived here in Pittsburgh has met someone for a date or business meeting under "The Clock". The cosmetics department sat in the center of the department store, where all of the action took place during lunch time.

The first cosmetics company that I worked for was "Borgesa". I still love the mud mask that came in a wide mouth glass mason jar. Then our manager told me of an opening at "Elizabeth

Arden's" counter. I was a little apprehensive, only because they hadn't quit developed a line for women of color and I wasn't sure if it would be a good fit for me. At that time the only cosmetic line that was specifically created for "African American" women was "Fashion Fair". Even they were still fine tuning their products, however they cornered the market at that time. Between the hours of 11am and 2pm the first floor would be packed! That is when you didn't have to hustle because of the lunch traffic, however you had to sell fast. That was the time to capitalize off of the high traffic. I could always multitask and I quick on my feet. I never wanted to take lunch during that time not only did we have a salary we received a commission draw base on our sales. And high volume sales always lead to bonuses and promotions. That was also the time when most of the single men of Pittsburgh would come though to check us out. Being in cosmetic sales sort of solidify you as being attractive. I took any opening that was available on the first floor. I even worked in the accessories department and we received discounts on any item in the store. Working there had great perks for a young woman who wanted to make connections, and it really helped to build one's wardrobe. I enjoyed it immensely. Those were days of nostalgia. The holidays came and I finally met Jerry's family together at his family home. They had a beautiful home in Fox Chapel, an upscale area of Pittsburgh. It smelled of Christmas diner and his siblings were coming in from out of town. I took it upon myself and brought his gifts over., however I didn't know it at the time that Jerry hadn't purchased me a thing. His family was very nice and tried to ignore that he hadn't., all except for his mother. She called him out, but not in front of everyone, however, I over heard her telling him that she didn't raise him like that. I could tell that Jerry was embarrassed. I know that his mother was and she would make sure that he made good of it. He came back in the living room where I was sitting and apologized and told me to met him at Saks Fifth Ave in the morning. His mother asked me to stay for a while and I did, only for a brief time. I had other stops to make. Christmas was my favorite holiday and still is, however I held Jerry to Saks.

He kept his word and we met there around lunch the next day. I wasn't too angry, I like to see a persons character early on. And since he didn't think of me before Christmas I was going to "Blow Up" his credit card. He was very patient and I tried on all sorts of things. I really enjoy after Christmas sales and I made my selections and took them to the register. We were all set until he pulled out his credit card…it wasn't his, it was his mothers. I declined to make all of those purchases at his mothers expense, and select one outfit. I wasn't completely finished holding him accountable, however his mother wasn't at fault. I grew much more fond of her and had a great deal of respect for how she raised her sons. The holidays were over and I was back to work this time in the accessories department and I notice my mother (who doesn't like to shop) coming down the escalator. What was she doing here I thought? Then I looked more closely and heard some commotion in the store. It was near closing time so thing were slowing down. Mostly at that time you would only hear the sounds of the coins being counted in the registers, so we could punch out in time to ensure that you would not miss your bus home. Most people in those days used public transportation to travel down town. It was just so convient.

As my mother was coming down the escalator, that was when I noticed that she was surrounded by the singing group "DeBarge". What was she doing with them and how did she know them I thought? (that was what all the commotion was all about). They would walk up to my counter and she had the biggest smile on her face. Actually they all were smiling and having a good time. When my mother visited Syreeta in Los Angeles about 2 years prior, she met a lot of Syretta's friends and a man named Skip. He became DeBarges Road manager and either they got in touch because of Syreeta and/ or he had my mothers contact information and followed up on his own. Nevertheless it benefited us. They were going to be in concert the following night and were staying at the "William Penn Hotel" across the street from my job. I was held up a bit from closing my register however, I wasn't concerned about missing my bus since my mom was there (she probably had driven down town and was parked somewhere near by). I had a young and cool manager named Grace and she offered to take my tallies upstairs so I could find out more information about the concert. After she came back I told her about it and invited her to come along. We could hardly wait and I told Grace that I'd see her first thing in the morning.

My mother and I would go across the street with the brothers and we sat in the lobby for just a few minuets, because of the growing number of fans surrounding the hotel it was much easier to retreat to their rooms. I ended up in the room with Marc and James. Their brother Randy kept asking me if I had some friends to invite over. I told him that I had sisters, however, I knew my baby sister was a little young for them and to be in this type of environment, besides she was about in the 10th grade. My mother went with their manager Skip and some other band members she met through Syreeta. One of the band members name was Jimmy Steward. He was a drummer and sweet as pie. In fact everyone was nice. Randy got board with us because I couldn't get in touch with my eldest sister at this time and he left the room. So that left Marc and James and myself. They seemed to be glad to have someone besides their brothers to talk to. They were easy and were gentlemen. We ordered room service, just burgers and fries nothing fancy, we were all kids. But sparks were flying between Marc and I. When we ate our food still talking a lot in-between bites James went looking for Randy. Marc and I talked so much so that I lost tract of time. Heck we both did. It was almost morning and I was concerned why hadn't my mother checked on me and where was she? Finally she came to Marc's room with both Skip and Jimmy. She said that we were going home and coming back later to see them in concert. I had a lot to do between now and then...go to work, see if I could get off early to get ready, and decide who I was going to take with me to the concert. Heck I needed witnesses! Marc and I hugged and could hardly wait to see each other later that day. Since my mothers father was a musician and was married to "Dinah Washington" my mother had grown up on music and the business of it and passed her love for it down to her children. As I watch the sun come up on our drive home she was just talking, and I couldn't hear a word that she was saying. I was hit by the "Love Bug" and could not process a word she was saying.

I tried to get an hour or two of sleep but couldn't. With all of the questions Lisa and Holly had like… "where were the two of you" and "what time is the concert" and "can we bring a friend"? So while I was answering all of their questions, I decided to get some breakfast and just get ready for work. Lisa was already on the phone lining up her friend Beth Anne to go with us. My mom told us only one friend each, she knew it might be tight back stage and knew they didn't need a "FRENZY". When I got to work I was bombarded with questions. Mostly about can I get them tickets. Today I was the most popular girl on the floor. I knew that I couldn't take them all and I never told anyone anything that I couldn't deliver on. So I told my manager Grace if she'd allow me to leave work early that I would let her be my plus one. Of course she agreed. We both left early and met up at the event. It was a big deal whenever celebrities came to a town like Pittsburgh. There wasn't internet or shows like "Entertainment Tonight" where you got a flood gate of information on them and how they lived.

We didn't have seats to watch the concert from. We were more up close. We stood back stage and watch them sing from the side of the stage. We were so excited and they were great in concert. They had beautiful voices and their songs were on the Top of the Charts. All of us girls kept looking at one another and kept grinning as if we were in disbelief that only 24 hours ago our lives were normal. What had taken place in that short amount of time? All I kept thinking is that I now had a different expectation of how my life could be…normalcy was out the door! After the show Grace thanked me and said that she had to leave. Since she was manager she had another set of responsibilities then I . She said that she'd understood and would give me grace if I were to come in late the next day. The rest of us went back to the hotel for food and more fun. Randy was glad this time I had my sister and her best friend Beth Anne. Believe it or not it wasn't a time where people just hooked up. Marc and I went to his room and along with James, he was a bit younger and wasn't that interested in girls that much until later when he would meet his future wife (Janet Jackson) of the famous "Jackson" family. Marc must have asked him to give us some privacy and so he left us alone in the room. Well, that didn't last very long and we got a knock at the door. It was El their brother who mostly sang lead. I recognized him right away and apparently so did he. I was the girl he recognized from the side of the stage. He wanted to know how Marc and I knew each other and where was he went all of this has taken place. I figured that he was a lot like my sisters sometimes when they thought they'd missed out on something. I guess Marc was hoping that I wouldn't explore that option and I had no desire. I was already satisfied with my choice. Lead singer or not, I wasn't going to fight the spark between Marc and I. I was going to let it take over and hopefully never let it go. El didn't stick around for long. He could see that the choice had been made. I would never come between brothers or friends for that matter. Besides, it would have cheapened me and any potential future for Marc and I. We stayed up most of the night talking and this time kissing. My goodness was Marc a good kisser. I had it bad, but we some how managed to fall asleep. The past 24 hours or more was very eventful. It was very sweet, we spooned and slept on top of the covers fully dressed until someone came and woke us. A few of the band members, Marc, Randy and I including Bethe Anne my mother and sister Lisa all went back to our house. I was glad for Marc to see where I lived and how I grew up, so he'd know I wasn't desperate and just liked him for himself. My mother was concerned what could she possibly cook to feed all of those men. And I by no means was going to help. Marc and I snuck off to my room and snuggled up in one of my twin bed much like we did at his hotel room. It was hard to sleep because of all the noise and commotion coming from the kitchen. We did come out for a brief moment to eat some of the waffles my mother had made and we snuck off again and by now this time I knew that I wasn't going to work. So I called Grace and she was kind enough to cover me. Not only that she was still excited about the concert and now had the floor to tell everyone at work her side of what happened. She was a very cool manager. Marc and I did manage to get a little sleep, but by afternoon our house was surrounded by neighborhood girls and some we knew from high school. The word had got around that "DeBarge" was inside our house. It was almost becoming riot like and they didn't have security in those days except for at the arena's and event places and if you were lucky hotel security, but not personal security. You had to be a "Jackson" or "Beatle"! So the next best thing we could think of was our local police department. Well, they have never heard of such a thing or DeBarge and told us this was a private matter, however, when some of our neighbors must have complained they had to drive by and dispersed the crowd. Now was the best time for them to leave and go back to the hotel. Besides, their tour had to continue and Marc and I looked like two love sick puppies. Or at least I was hoping he felt the same as I did. And it was very mutual. We would exchange phone numbers and addresses, but that didn't do me any good. What he gave me was his address and phone number in Detroit where they were from. He only had his touring schedule and could only call me when he arrived to the hotels and then he had rehearsals and travel in between time from city to city. I know that this would be difficult for younger people to comprehend to live without cell phones and for the first time in life I'd wish that we could have had one. It would have made life easier for every one including their manager Skip. When he got all of those huge phone bills from the hotels, he had to reach out to my mother and let her know. Well, she knew already...I was sitting by the phone as much as possible and asked my sisters to intervene should I missed any of Marc's calls. The crazy thing was that we couldn't even give ourselves a time to be by the phone. We could only estimate. They never knew if their bus would get to the next city on time or should they have to stop for gas or to eat. It wasn't an ideal way to date. However, when we did talk it was for hours at a time. Thank goodness for my job, it became my diversion. I became quite annoyed by all the chatter at work because it only made me think of Marc even more. We'd miss each other terribly. I was glad to get a call from their manager Skip. He had contacted my mother after about a month and told her about the huge phone bills and that they knew it was Marc. My mothers phone number was on the bill at least one hundred times and that he'd thought it would be more economical to get us together and that they'd soon be pro-forming in Cleveland, Ohio which was only a 2 hour drive away from Pittsburgh and invited us to come up. There is a God I thought, our prayers have been answered or our persistency of longing to be together.

I didn't know it at the time that my mother had two different agenda's for wanting to take me. The first had nothing to do with me seeing Marc at all. My older brother got caught riding in a stolen vehicle and was being detained in Cleveland. His friend Joey had taken Joey's uncles car and his uncle reported Joey and my brother was riding with Joey at the time. So my mother never said a word to us about what happened to Stanley and let Stanley stay in the detention centre for a few days before she would get him out, so he'd learn his lesson. I was glad to have any excuse for us to go and in the meantime we picked up Stanley. My mother didn't want to reward him with a front row seat to the concert, however she hadn't much of a choice. They played at a stadium that circled around on the floor so that everyone could have a great view. It made me kind of dizzy watching and I was a bit concerned for them hoping that they weren't getting dizzy as well. Their sister Bunny pro-formed with them that night and that was the first time that I got to meet her. She was beautiful and classy soft spoken and gracious. They'd just seemed to have their act together. After the show Marc and

Randy got in the car with my mother myself, and brother Stanley. We rode this time to a motel where they were staying. (this is a piece of information for the fans who think that life on the road is always glamorous). Stanley would run off somewhere with Randy and my mother would catch up with Skip. They weren't dating or anything like the sort I believe Skip was homosexual and it wasn't popular and most choose to live in the closet. It was just easier and sometimes safer. They just developed a friendship when my mother was out west visiting Syreeta. Marc and I were in the hallway when we ran into El. He wasn't as friendly as he was when we first met back in Pittsburgh. He knew that Marc and I were keeping in touch, heck everyone on their tour knew. Especially because of the racket Skip made over the expensive phone bills. We didn't pause for conversation with El and went straight in Marc's room. This time we were all alone no brothers as if he'd made prior arrangements with them Hind sight he'd probably did and I didn't care...I wanted very much to be alone with him as well. At first we kissed and hugged for a very long time in the silence. The kisses were very passionate but our hugs were as friends, very long and tight embraces. We had missed each other as if we were friends much longer than the short amount of time from when we first met. He started to slowly remove my clothes, so slow that he was making sure that I had enough time to tell him to stop, but I never said a word. We slid under the covers and he made love to me. I wasn't concerned about anything, not even my mother coming to find me. In fact no one came to bother us. They probably all knew and left us alone. It was SWEET. The moment felt as if we were on our Honeymoon. We laid there in the silence of the night, I wasn't afraid of being in any sort of trouble with my mother or his manager. When we did speak it was about getting together a plan to be with each other as soon as possible. We knew that they would be off to another city and I back to Pittsburgh and Marc told me that he had no more tour date near Pittsburgh and after the tour he'd be back in California. We spooned some more and got up early the following morning and ate breakfast with the rest of everyone. No one asked us or said a thing.

The band was packing up the bus and Marc and I sat there without a sure plan in place. The thought of having not to see him and wait for phone calls was making me sad in advance. So when they were packing up Marc hid me on the bus. My mother was saying goodbye and I guess assumed that I'd got in the car so no one would see me cry. They started up the bus and pulled off. By the time my mother reached her car and got in she knew I was on the bus. Of course she flagged them down and Skip knew right away what was left behind…ME. We were like children and weren't quit adults and Marc and his brothers didn't have charge over their own money. In those times they had management for all those sorts of things. Especially when your fresh out the gate. Well, I cried all the way back to Pittsburgh and my brother couldn't understand and he'd never seen me like this before. I had never been in love before, and at least he had the since not to tease me. I went straight back to work.

Jerry would come around my job from time to time . He wasn't sure just why he hadn't seen me in a while and I didn't tell him. I am sure that he knew. Not a lot of exciting things happened at that time in Pittsburgh besides our football team. However, I didn't want to be bothered with him and I wasn't looking forward to waiting around for another rondavious' on tour. Mark would call as much as possible and talked Skip into letting me visit when they got to Miami. We spent most of our time on the beach holding hands. But Marc never gave me a plan for when he would get back to LA. When I returned to Pittsburgh the cosmetic company that I worked for (Elizabeth Arden) had an opening at their "Red Door" salon on Rodeo Drive in BeverlyHills. Only thing, the position wasn't for a few months and I still had to interview for it. Besides I could stay with Syreeta I thought. Fat chance, word had gotten back to her about Marc and I were carrying around and she wasn't going to be responsible for me possibly getting pregnant…no Mame, not on her watch. Mommy told her that I wasn't going to take no for an answer and that I was going to make a way somehow and that I already had a job lined up. So mommy and Syreeta came up with a plan of their own and if there was anybody who could keep a watch over me was "Aunt Essie", Syreeta's church going Mother. Nothing had ever got past Aunt Essie, she was as stern as they come. I didn't care who they came up with in order to get me to California I just wanted to go. They spoke with Aunt Essie about it and to my surprise she was in agreement with it. Aunt Essie never met a challenge that she couldn't beat...well so she thought!

This time I had gotten on my mothers last nerve and she asked me to move out right before my time came to leave Pittsburgh. I stayed with my mothers friend Willa Mae's husband Eddie in Penn Hills. It was ok because we had lived with them before when I was in the 7th grade when our house caught on fire. We stayed with them for almost a year while the insurance company re-build our house. The only fault in my plan is that I hadn't yet received the position with Elizabeth Arden as of yet and Marc was keeping a secret. I only stay a few weeks at Uncle Eddies and a few days before my departure I got a call from Jerry. He wanted to give me some last resort send off. I hadn't thought much about him since I stared seeing Marc. I agreed and we went to a spot in "East Hills". I told one of my friends named Essie (not to be confused with my Aunt Essie) to meet us there. I wore all white except for a colorful red scarf around my waste. I wound up having a pretty good time. I danced a lot and had a few drinks. Not enough to be drunk, especially since the time I did at college. I didn't like feeling out of sorts. We stayed until the club was closed and afterwards Jerry rode me back to Uncles Eddie's house and I could tell that he didn't want to leave. So we walked around to the back of the house and sat out back. Jerry asked if we could go skinny dipping in my Uncles pool. It was a hot summer evening so I agreed on one thing that I would not get fully undressed, but he did. I didn't care if there was 100 naked men in the pool I was in love with Marc and that was that...but I wasn't so sure that Marc still shared the same feelings for me. I didn't want Jerry to get close to me for a few different reasons. I didn't want to lead him on and two I didn't want to wet my hair because I didn't have time to do it again before my flight in the morning. I don't think that Jerry really believed that I was going anywhere. But he would shock me with a last minuet proposal. He whipped out this pear shaped diamond ring on a gold band and asked me not to leave. I was shocked. He told me his sister Gina (aka Bonnie) helped him pick it out. I couldn't believe that he even had a plan and when did he come up with this and how come men wait until your about to do something drastic before they try and make for a real relationship? I had no clue at all. Not that it changed anything for me. I'd rather take a chance on California with all of it's missing parts than to marry someone only because he used a ring as a last effort resort. I would leave in the morning.

It was the longest flight in history. Prior to that I had not flown much. Besides I had too much on my mind. On one hand I was excited and on the other I had reservations. One being I was staying with Aunt Essie and two Marc didn't seem to be to excited that I was on my way and three, I hadn't yet interview for my new position. And the interview wasn't for another month so what was I going do for an income besides my savings that I had with me.

It was one of the most beautiful sights I had ever seen before. Landing on the sunniest day that I had ever witnessed. The airport was enormous compared to the one in Pittsburgh and so many people going to-and-fro. When I was coming down the jet way I had a thought…I hadn't seen Aunt Essie in a while…what did she look like? Well, there she was looking like "Sit tin Bull". Aunt Essie was a big strappin woman with beautiful red brown skin and huge breast and long "Ponca Honua's" ponytails. She looked the same and she recognized me right away. She gave me a big hug and kiss and never asked me about my flight, she just immediately asked me…"Child, what ever happened to all your hair"? I had forgotten that a few nights before that I let my friend Veronica put in a relaxer and it all came out. I kind of liked myself with short hair. I believe it started a new trend the wrap! We went to baggage claim and got my trunk and put it in Aunt Essie's hunter green Volvo. She was just talking away and my eyes were all over the place. I was admiring all of the Palm Trees. They were every where and all of the tropical plants. Flowers that I have never seen before or just a few when I had my brief time in Miami with Marc. Aunt Essie had mentioned something about having to drop off at Kim's house. I had forgotten all about Kim. She was the daughter my Aunt Essie adopted a long time ago and she was my age…good, now I would have someone to hang out with to show me around when Marc was busy or in the studio. We would swing by Kim's house and then I thought to myself why did Kim have her own place with her being so young. Well, my question was answered quickly when we pulled up. Kim looked as if she were going to burst at the seams. She was about nine months pregnant and married…well,there goes my plans right out the window. She was glad to see me for what was to be expected. It was hot and she looked over due! I tried to appear happy for her, but all I could think of is what my mother always tried to keep us from, was now happening to her. What could we possibly have in common to talk about anymore…

We only stay for a few minuets and Aunt Essie wanted to get me home so she could make diner and go over the rules for me. I knew them all, they would be the same rules as my mother taught me. And since she and Syreeta grew up together right in the same block, I knew that I wasn't in for no party. The only difference between them and me is that I wasn't afraid of Aunt Essie. I knew that she wasn't a push over, but what I did know she had been young once, and had to been in love once before how else would Syreeta have gotten here.

We ate baked chicken and white rice and steamed broccoli which was a diner staple at her house, so was listening to Rev. Price at the diner table. The food was very bland. Aunt Essie was watching her salt intake amongst other things. She was cooking for her health. That was an LA thing—eating healthy. We turned in early, I slept on the couch, when I could hear her snoring I thought of Marc and how I imagine our first encounter would be. He didn't know that I even arrived yet. The next day was for errands. That was the first time I saw a "Trader Joe's". The produce in the stores looked picture perfect. Every thing in California was a new discovery, I was in a new place. And much like New York LA was multi-cultural. The only difference is New York Hispanic culture was made up of Porter Ricans and Dominican's and LA was mostly Mexican's. I knew that my great great grand mother on my mother side was Mexican, but I didn't have any pictures of her. She is buried with my great great grand father on the campus of Alabama A&M University. Her name was Maria Howard Councill. She was the founders wife. I was tired of walking around and Aunt Essie was so picky and took 15 minuets for her to choose one piece of fruit. I wished that she would at least take me by Syreeta's house so I could go swimming and see her two boys Jamal and his brother Hodari who were kept by their nanny when Syreeta wasn't at home. They were young and either I'd just be baby sitting them which I didn't mind, but I still had no one my age to hang out with. Aunt Essie had other plans for me. She thought it would be great for me to drive her around on her errands, except one problem I didn't have a valid drivers license. So Aunt Essie put that next on our to do list. When we showed up at the DMV in Los Angeles it was packed. Just an ordinary day there, the lines looked as if they never stopped, some even went out the door. I would take a number and get in line and we both sat down. I couldn't believe that Aunt Essie would be so patient and do something so nice for me. I wasn't her child however, she knew that I needed ID and some independence out here. I didn't past the written exam on the first try only because I assumed the laws would be much like Pittsburgh. I had to wait 24 hours before I could take it again. So I took the pamphlet home and studied. Aunt Essie wasn't going to take me back until I was ready, she wasn't going to allow anyone to waste her time, not even me.

We would return about 3 days or so. The lines weren't as bad as before and since I was already there a few days ago I got in fast. I past this time and signed up for the driving portion. Since they had an opening we waited. I had never driven outside of Pittsburgh before. Nothing was familiar, no land marks so I had to focus. We used Aunt Essie's Volvo and she stayed back at the DMV they only allowed the student and drivers aid. That was perfect for me I didn't need her there to make me nervous. I put on my seat belt and adjusted all of the mirrors and then proceeded out of the parking lot where he instructed me to make a right. We had only driven about 3 blocks down the street and every time I got to an intersection I would pause only because I wasn't familiar with the streets and not because I had a stop sign. Well, someone had run the stop sign at the 4 way intersection and if it hadn't been for me stopping, they would have killed me and the instructor. He was pretty shaken up. He told me to pull over and he was shaking when he was writing something down on my form. He told me to turn around and go back to the DMV. I thought that I'd done something wrong, he said no you saved us all from an accident by driving safe and past me without further testing! Boy was I happy and Aunt Essie was too, this gave her confidence that I would be a safe driver. She insisted that I drive us home.

I needed to do something for myself and Aunt Essie gave me the want ads of the Sunday paper, she said find a job. That was fine by me. I liked keeping busy and I hadn't any privacy in her small one bedroom apartment to contact Marc. I couldn't let Aunt Essie think I came all the way out here for a man who I wasn't sure what his intentions were. Besides she would have told me to let him pay for your move and she would have been right. That would be one of the first mistakes I could remember making for a man. I found a "want ad" for a receptionist position in "Century City" for an Accounting Firm called "Kenneth Levinthal and Co". I held one other previous receptionist position for a brief time in Pittsburgh. It mostly consist of greeting prospective clients and guest. Seating them in a nearby conference room and offering them something to drink, then notifying whom ever that they were there. It helped even more if you were somewhat attractive. Some company's liked for their prospective clients to associate an attractive face with the company when they first arrive. Sounds a little silly, however if you watch some old "Turner Classic's Movies" you'd see that often. I got up the next morning very early and dressed conservatively and took the bust down Sunset Blvd until I got to "Century City". The bus system was much easier than Pittsburgh. Most buses went north to south and east to west, and they made a PA announcement at all main stops. Much before its time. I was familiar with the towers, it was similar to the ones in New York. They were located on the 17th floor and I met with one of the managers who did the hiring for that department. She liked me and hired me on the spot. I was introduced around to some of the employee's who weren't busy as of yet. I went home to tell Aunt Essie the good news and that I would start in the morning.

One thing about the bus, you would kind of get to know people who had the same daily routine. The next day I got off at my stop and took the crowded evaluator to the 17th floor. I was introduced to a lady named Cora who was the main switch board operator. If you don't know what that is just watch some old movies on "Turner Classic Movie" channel. It's a small room not to much larger that the average closet. She was a pro. That thing seemed to have over a hundred different outlets to it. How did she know which outlet would connect to the right person. She had memorized them all. She could connect calls at the rate of a computer. I would mostly work the front desk and that made me happy, only because Cora didn't have a formula for all of the madness of that contraption she mastered. It was only in her head. Thank goodness she never took a day off, except one day that she got sick and there was no one to cover her but me. I knew that I didn't have a clue and when the markets were open on the East coast that thing would go haywire! Finally the manager of our department and took over for me, I was dropping calls like a greasy piglet. She must have received complaints from some of the partners and jumped in before they lost perspective clients. It wasn't my fault, even the partners couldn't master that thing that's why Cora was so valuable to them. She should have asked for more compensation. There were only four of us (African Americans) working there at the time. It was Cora, a guy named Jeffrey, (that worked in the mail department) myself, and a new hire accountant named Wanda Ford. She was closer to my age and very professional. One day I went to her office and asked her to go to lunch with me on my break. We went to an outdoor eatery that was between the two towers and learned a great deal about each other. She came from a good family back in Houston, Texas and lived here in LA with her sister, niece and nephew. She drove a cute two seater car and we became good friends over the years to come. Jeffrey was another person who I got to know as well. That was one thing about being people of color in any work environment, we'd gravitate towards one another for comfort and support, especially when there aren't many of you. Also it was an unwritten code. One day Jeffrey offered me a ride home, I only said yes because it took so long for the bus and some times they were so crowded that you would have to wait for the next one. We stopped off at "Fat Burgers" it was a popular fast food eatery that is mostly exclusive to the Los Angelo's area. I'm not sure which of the times he would ride me to my cousins apartment, his name was Damian. He was Aunt Essie's nephew, her sister Rosa Lee son (Rosa Lee was my Aunt Lois's best friend back in Pittsburgh. Aunt Lois' house was where we moved into when we came back from New York). When we got to Damian's apartment I was a little taken back. It was one of those furnished places where everything was made from the same materials. He was glad to see me and how much I grew up. Damian always liked having pretty girls around it helped him get the things that he wanted. Damian worked in the music business and got his feet in the door from our cousin Syreeta being she was a well known writer and ex-wife of Stevie Wonder. (Damian and Syreeta's mothers were sisters). I couldn't tell you what he actually did for Stevie to this very day. He didn't play an instrument sing or wasn't a sound engineer or anything of the sort. I think he was the party man who set up things for people. Not to taint Steve's reputation none the least, Stevie was straight lace much like myself, his only vice was women and chocolate chip cookies and he wasn't by himself, most of celebrities rolled like that. It just came with the territory, not the cookies but the women.

Debra, senior year, class of 1982 Penn Hills High School.

Debra senior year Miss Black Teenage Pageant (1982)
with pageant director Jean Bryant.

76   Debra modeling for Kaufmann's Department Store,
Pittsburgh. (1983)

Dorm shirts for your special Valentine

Debra and Brian on their way to college.
Washington D.C., Summer of 1982.

Aunt Essie, Syretta's mother, who Debra lived with upon moving to California.

Charlotte, Debra's mother, at home with Stevie Wonder.

Marc DeBarge (the singing group DeBarge) with Debra's 81
mother Charlotte after a concert in Cleveland, Ohio.

El DeBarge and Debra in Pittsburgh, PA.

At home on Sunset Plaza Drive. Debra with best friend Lynn, and Jim's daughter Kimberly.

84   Jim Brown and Debra in
the Hall of Fame Parade in Canton, Ohio.
Reprinted with permission from The (Canton) Repository

Jim and Debra along with two fans 85
at Hall of Fame Luncheon in Canton, Ohio.
Reprinted with permission from The (Canton) Repository

Event Page - Canton Repository 8-4-86

Brunch rings down curtain on HOF Festival

Former Cleveland Browns football star Jim Brown signs autographs for Cynthia Conley (left) and Sheila Cherry (center), as his fiancee, Debra Clark, joins in the conversation. Brown, a 1971 Pro Football Hall of Fame cashinee, attended the 12th annual Hall of Fame Champagne Brunch Sunday, before he and Miss Clark returned to California. (Repository staff photo) (Story and more photos on Page 3)

86 Debra and Jim on the set of the movie *The Running Man*, in which Jim had a starring role.

Leading man Arnold Schwartsenaeger and Jim Brown and 87 other cast members on set for the movie *The Running Man*.

Jim Brown and best friend George Hughley at a fundraiser.

Jim and Debra at Syracuse University where Jim was   89
being recognized as a prestegious alumni.

Jim and Debra's first day in Hawaii.

Jim and Debra at local eatery.

Debra working as flight attendant for Continental Airlines 103

94 BethAnne Anderson, Debra's friend, who didn't survive
    domestic violence and for whom this book is dedicated.

I was tired and fell asleep on Damian couch. Jeffrey and Damian were still talking. Damian was very street slick or another term "Street Wise". He had Jeffrey figured out from the door. Jeffrey knew how to get his hands on a few things and Damian knew how to con. While Jeffrey made a run and Damien went into my purse while I was asleep and took my whole fresh stack of money from my wallet. I had just gotten paid. When Jeffrey returned, Damien would go in the bathroom to enjoying his purchase. Jeffrey woke me up and said lets go. I wanted to freshen up before we left but Damian wouldn't come out of the bathroom for me to use it. Jeffrey was trying to explain that he'd wouldn't be coming out for quit some time. When I went in my purse to get my compact out to check myself I notices that my money was missing. I knew that it wasn't Jeffrey because he had just gotten paid too along with me and he wanted to date me and wouldn't have a reason to rob me so using the process of illumination, the culprit was Damian. I went completely off! I didn't care who the hell it was, no one was going to take advantage of me period! Damian was in a state of paranoia and didn't want the police to be called because he was in no state to be around any authority. I could figure what took place so Jeffrey took me to his car and explained to me that he didn't know where Damian had gotten the money from. And that Damian must have gone into my purse when Jeffrey left to get Damian's stuff. Jeffrey gave me back some of the money but not all of it because he had to pay someone for the stuff. I was mad as hell and didn't care either way I wasn't ever going to trust neither of them period! Jeffrey would try and make things up to me however, I wasn't interested non the least. I only allowed him to take me to eat and ride me home if I didn't want to wait for the bus. But that was all he would ever be to me from that point on was a ride. My friend Wanda who worked with us at Kenneth Leventhal told me later that Jeffrey purchased a huge ring and bracelet for me. He thought that would make it up to me. He showed it to her at work. She later told me it was beautiful. I believed her, Wanda had great taste.

The position would finally open up at Elizabeth Arden. I was glad about it and set up the time for my interview. I was to meet with the salon head manager Ms. Saundra Scofield. I was so excited and knew exactly the location being I rode past Rodeo Dr everyday on my way to work in Century City. She had heard great things about me from my previous manager in Pittsburgh, and I made a good impression with my grooming or so I thought. It was great for Pittsburgh, however not so good for BeverlyHills. She was a very smart woman but not what I had expected for the beauty industry. She was average looking and dressed as if she worked in an office of some sort. She looked as if she'd make a great accountant where I'd just come from. She asked me where did I see myself in 10 years and I replied…"exactly where you're seated". So dumb and arrogant of me. The reason why she sat in that seat was very obvious to me now, she had wisdom. Wisdom enough not to be threatened by some young but very ambitiously driven inexperienced young girl. Instead she offered to show me the ropes and give me a shot. I got the job. I gave Kenneth Leventhal my two week notice and I was out of there. I assumed that they were glad to see me go, I had no future with an accounting firm and the only thing we could do for each other was part ways…adiós amigos!

My first day on the job was very exciting for me. I was introduced to everyone and every department. I was in my element and very happy to be there, although I could see the expression on a few employees that weren't that happy to see me. I wasn't sure what their deal was and it wasn't important to me. I had gotten the desired position that I had come out to LA for, so my move wasn't entirely a total bust. I though they just had to get to know me, there wasn't but one other African American person that worked there besides the people in the domestic positions, janitorial, house keeping and the ones who prepared the lunches for clients who came for a full day of pampering. But before I got started I was given a complete make over from massage, pedicure and complete body waxing. I was a little stubborn about my mustache, but glad that they persist. That was a Pittsburgh thing. To this day it bothers me to see that on a woman. I would start fresh the next day. I put on my finest of clothes for my first day. I had a very nice wardrobe from my modeling days at all of the department stores back in Pittsburgh, but nothing in comparison to BeverlyHills. The only thing comparable is Paris France and Fifth Ave in New York. I was back on the bus since I wasn't working with Jeffrey anymore and didn't care. I met a young lady while riding the bus to work named Cindy. She was a professional who did some sort of secretarial position and wore smart suits and dresses to work, a real genteelly Southern Belle from New Orleans, La. Cindy was soft and girly and very attractive. She and I would sit together most mornings. I would try to save her a seat on the bus. She was about my age maybe a few years older , however a lot more mature. Southern girls always seemed more mature to me. They carried themselves much like women. She told me that she had seen me on the bus before and because it was always so crowded we didn't have an opportunity to talk. She had a one bed room apartment on West Norton Street, smack dab in the middle of "West Hollywood" which seemed a bit strange to me because everyone knew it was the hottest spot for gay men. I thought she'd never get a date living there. I wasn't thinking it would be the safest place for a single girl. No one would bother you, they were there for the hot guys, a girl was perfectly safe in West Hollywood. Actually it was a very smart move. After a few of our conversations she made me an offer to become her roommate and I was glad to have met my first friend my age with something in common even if it was just sharing her apartment. I wanted freedom and no way was I going to bring Marc to Aunt Essie's apartment. She probably would have liked him, however there was just no privacy for us. I gave Aunt Essie the news and she wished me the best, next thing I knew I had a place, not all of my own, but I thought I was well on my way…

I loved my new job, however, I wasn't doing a lot of make overs mostly due to no one wanted to test out the new girl. So

I became mainly a floater and would fill in for people who took their lunch breaks, or if someone got sick and called off. Funny the one thing that I didn't want to have done to me is what I became very good at, waxing. The Russian women were pros and one of the skin care estheticians named Ebie would show me the ropes. She was beautiful, something out of a "James Bond" movie, She had an accent that sounded like Yolanda Foster and was very womanly. One day I got an emergency page on the inter-call that I was wanted in the hair salon. What ever would they want of me I thought. So I immediately went to the salon department and there were two victims sitting with their hair all bunched in a complete knot! It was two African American women who's husbands gave them a full day of beauty and a trip to California, and not many of us came to places in those days and the hair stylist was panache to say the least. He whispered to me and said…their hair was straight before I shampooed it and then it turned into that…I asked him if he'd had any conditioner with a heavy amount of moisture and/ or cellophane based conditioning product and he did. I applied it to both of their hair and put them under the dryer to buy some time and give him the rest of instructions to complete their hair. I explained to him that their hair must have been pressed out with heat and when he washed it , their hair reverted back to it's natural state. And since he had no pressing comb he would have to blow dry their hair as straight as he could get it and turn his curling iron up to straighten out the rest. It will help if he set the curls in a roller while he was curling sections as he went. And to first comb the hair out with the conditioner still in it and then rinse. I saved the day and earned his trust.

The weekend was here and I thought it would be a good time to finally call Marc. The number he gave me was for El's house. I didn't care I was just glad to hear his voice and he seemed to be the same. He immediately came over and I had the place to myself. Cindy was on a date or something. She was sort of a serial dater. I wasn't jealous or any thing I just couldn't figure out how or if she was truly interested in that many men. It wasn't any of my business anyhow. She was a good room mate and opened up her doors to me. God put some good people in my path along the way. She even sometime had breakfast dates, I'm not kidding. I would watch her get picked up in the morning and after work she'd come home with a doggie bag after work and still remained thin! She said it saved her on groceries.

It was time…Marc was on his way and I was home alone except for Cindy's cat named Dreyfus who wasn't very fawn of me and neither I was fawned of him. I cleaned up the place and didn't cook anything, I didn't want to seemed to anxious for his arrival. I made sure that I looked casually cute not to over do. When I opened the door it was like no time had ever past between us. We hugged for a long time and he always gave me a very long and passionate kiss. We sat on the sofa and caught up. He wanted to know when did I get there and how come I never contacted him until now. I had only been there a little over a month, but when you care for someone and hadn't spoken about any plans I wanted to make sure it was safe for my heart. Although he looked the same he was behaving a little different. He seemed to have something bothering him and I could tell it wasn't me. I seemed to be a comfort for him and not the problem. Any how he used the bathroom and then asked if he could take a shower. Not the kind to wash off another woman but to wash off a problem and sort things out. At that time he wouldn't share with me what was bothering him. They were working on their second album and I guess in negotiations with Motown and the business aspects of it all. He seemed to be under a lot of pressure. I didn't want to push to find out. We would retreat to Cindy's room being my bed was the pull out couch without a door for privacy. Afterwards we did our usual spooning and he fell asleep before I did. I couldn't fall asleep knowing that Cindy might return home and find us there in her bed. Not only that I was concerned for Marc. With all of the success that he and his brothers were having I could not figure out why he didn't seem happy. After he slept we got up and walked around the corner to "El Polo Loco".

We came back to the apartment and Cindy was back from her date. She was a bit taken back probably relieved to know that I wasn't a liar and made up the story about knowing Marc and his brothers. Her date left and Cindy stayed up with us for a little while and then she turned in. Marc spent the night with me on the pull out sofa. We just held each other, he seemed to need it more than I did. Any how I was grateful to see him. They next day he would leave and things were fine between us and I needed to prepare for work the next day. Sundays were always the time for me to do laundry and getting my clothes ready for the following week. Cindy was like that too. My weeks would be much of the same at work and home, not much of all the excitement I thought I would have in "Hollywood". Not even a cat fight between my gay neighbors and their lovers. One of my neighbors who lived downstairs from us was what I would think of as a cliché. He was a plump drag queen who worked at a local florist and had a skinny lover. His apartment was full of exotic flower arrangements of all sorts. He would fix me a cocktail and go on about his lover and his work. He reminded my of Robin Williams' lover in the movie "The Bird Cage". I don't know if Cindy ever spent much time with them, however, she had many more dates than I did. Besides a few of my family members were gay and I was used to hanging around them. I was glad to have the company and he was very entertaining. I wouldn't see Marc on a regular as much as I wanted to. Sometimes it was studio stuff and other times I wasn't so sure. Well, this weekend me and Cindy planned to go out ourselves. We heard about a new club opening up called "24 Karat", it was in West Hollywood and was a huge warehouse with the best Dj who had a New York sound. We had a ball and I was glad to now know where we could go for fun. One day after I had gotten paid and I ventured over to one of the stores near by and I ran into a girl named Niecy. She was working there and I knew of her from Pittsburgh. She told me that she and her friend Lynn had moved out there together and would love to hang out sometime. I told her about the new club and that it was a lot of fun. We exchanged phone numbers and I purchased a skirt from her and went home. I

got a call later sometime that week and it was Damian and I asked
him how did he know where I was, he told me Aunt Essie gave
him my number and he wanted me to come by when I could. I was
done with him after he stole my money, but Damian had his ways
of convincing you. I told him ok, but not until the weekend I had
to work. He told me that he had a new spot and gave me his new
address, he was closer by in West Hollywood too, just a little north
of where I was staying.

When the weekend came I went to see him and had my guard
up for his shenanigans. He act as if none of that had even taken
place. His new place was a replica of the last only darker. He never
would open up the curtains. Maybe afraid for someone to see what
really was going on. He wanted me to go with him to see Stevie at
the studio. I said ok and off we went to "Wonderland". Stevie was
very sweet and glad to meet me. He knew my mother because she
went to he and Syreeta's wedding back in Detroit. My mother would
see him when she came to visit Syreeta as well. He would always give
us contacts when someone was coming in concert in Pittsburgh that
was how I mostly got all of the back stage passes from him. We also
met one other time before when he performed in Pittsburgh at the
"Civic Arena". He was a bit of a jokester and light hearted. He told
me make myself at home so I did. I listened to his creations and
he was/is so very talented. I was in my element…MUSIC! Damian
introduced me to so many people…Aquill, Elizabeth and an up and
coming drummer from Philadelphia named Donnell Spencer. He
was near my age and that was the nice thing about Stevie he would
give new artist a try or at least allow them to sit in on a session or
two. Elizabeth and I would hit it off right away. She was petite much
like me, she was an aspiring actress and a lot of fun. She did a lot of
side work with T.V studio work, much assistant work for shows like
the "Grammy's". She was very out going and would be someone I'd
go to church with and hang out at "Wonderland" with. I believe she
was one of Steve's girls.

I met a lot of people though Damian. One who I become good friends with named Monique Brown. She was younger that I was and was from Bakersfield C.A. She was cute as a button. She reminds me of the girl Poe on "La La Anthony's Reality Show". Funny thing Damian didn't think we would get along, not so I got pretty close to her and we would stay in touch for a while after I left California. She introduced me to "New Edition" who were staying in the same hotel as Damian. There were a lot of up and coming celebrities who lived there, "Tears for Fears" was another one of many I could remember. Monique at the time had a crush on Ronnie. And for those who always blamed Bobby Brown for Whitney's drug use they lied. I saw those guys almost everyday for at least 4 months and the only thing I've know for any of them to do is maybe smoke a little pot. And I didn't witness much of that either. Just thought I'd just throw that in there. One day while Monique and I was hanging out with "New Edition's" Michael Bivans. He asked me where could we go and hang out. I told him about the new club that I had been to and how much fun I had. So we agreed to go that coming Friday, and his body guard Jeffrey(not to be confused with the Jeffrey I worked with at Kenneth Leventhal) would take us there. I would return that Friday to go out. Monique helped me with my hair. She was very skilled in that department. When she did her hair and makeup she looked like a little starlet! I was ready and Michael and Jeffrey picked me up. I didn't expect for us to look like a date with Jeffrey driving and Michael and I riding in the back seat of the limo. I didn't care I was in my first limo in "Hollywood"! We pulled up to the club and it was packed one of the longest line without there being a concert or something. It was a typical night at the club. Because of Michaels celebrity we got right through to the private parking area to be escorted to the front door, except when we got to the front door, Michael was turned away because of his age. I wasn't much older that he was but the rules were always different for girls, so I had a decision to make and fast, go in or leave with Michael…

Of course I went in the club. That music was sounding too good not to have gone in, and besides Michael wasn't my type or in my age category. Every one was there. Sheila E, LaToya Jackson, Micky Free, and the not yet discovered Vanessa Bell (Calloway) along with her long time friend Lela Rochon(who would later be feature in two of Eddie Murphy's future movies), and OH MY GOODNESS, "EDDIE MURPHY"!!! He was defiantly "A list". He just wrapped up BeverlyHills Cop 1. Long before Vanessa would star in his movie "Coming to America". I don't believe they even knew each other at that time. It was all new to all of us. I was so excited, it seemed as if ALL the stars we lining up in my favor. On my way to the bath room to make sure that I was looking good like most women do, especially since the stakes were so high that night. Eddie was HOT HOT HOT, in every sense of the word. Even Vanessa and her crew were in the bathroom. Every where you'd walk it was standing room only. I walked to the back bar when I came out of the bathroom and Micky Free called me over. We had met when he toured with the singing group "Shalimar" with Jody Watley and Howard Hewitt. They, too, were very popular. Micky was simply just pretty. He made women feel ugly but not me. I was confident and maybe a bit to much, but life has a way of evening out the score. Nevertheless, I stopped to chat with Micky, he was fun and full of compliments. He had a way of making you feel as if you are the only one in the room. While Micky had my undivided attention, from out of no where came Niecy and Lynn from Pittsburgh. We screamed like teenaged girls. Now if we planned this, it would have never happened and that was true. How could we all have shown up at the same time. I introduced them to Micky and we kept chatting about…"when did you come out to LA and where are you staying". I told Lynn that I ran into Niecy at her job while I was out shopping. While we were chatting it up I could see Niecy's facial expression changing, she had a look of shock on her face. It was Eddie Murphy and he was headed towards our way however he stopped for a minuet and said something to Mickey. Micky said that Eddie asked him if he (Micky) and I were together, and Mickey told him no. Well, Eddie wasn't coming our way but my way. He came over to me and asked me to dance. Lynn had the biggest smile on her face and Niecy had the usual look of "Hateration"! He took me to the center of the dance floor, which seemed like for ALL to see. I couldn't believe it, out of all the girls I was his choice. For some reason I secretly knew it. Remember before I said that I felt like all of the stars were lined up, it wasn't stars I know it was God and He was blessing me. I know that it might sound vain, but everyone that I met in "Hollywood" thought I was an actress or trying to be. It just wasn't my thing. I enjoyed what I did for a living and have for most of my career. I enjoy making women be at their best. Eddie was trying to have a conversation out on the dance floor and I wan't having it…I LOOOVEEED to dance. I was breaking it down and the music was so good the Dj was playing my song "Didn't mean to turn you on"! I just wanted to dance until my song was over, and in a few minuets it was. The Dj would slow it down to a slow song and Eddie didn't ask to keep dancing we just did. I couldn't believe it, I am slow dancing with the "hottest" man in Hollywood and no one would believe that this night is going down like this for me and then I remembered I had two witnesses from back home Niecy and Lynn. Too bad there were no cell phones at that time, but gossip of this sort would travel fast! After we danced he asked for me to come back to his table. He was sitting up and away from the crowd. It was much like a large bleacher in a stadium with more landing space for small size cafe tables. I was happy to be there talking with him however, it was difficult to hear. The music was very loud and the club was packed. After he offered me a drink (soft drink only) because he didn't drink alcohol, so he thought that was what I should have as well. I thought to myself "Bye Felicia". If he was making decisions for me this early I knew he would not be good for me long term. No one likes being controlled. I was always looking for signs, I was seeking but I didn't know what. Looking back I was glad that Eddie had choose me to dance and talk to that evening, however, I didn't need the validation. I had the normal amount of super sized inflated ego of a teen ager. So I told Eddie that I needed to check on my friend Micky and that it was nice to meet him and went back to where Micky and I were standing. Micky was interested in what Eddie had to say to me. I don't know what he'd expected. It was as normal as any conversation that I've had with any young man. I went to the lady's room again to check on my makeup. Since I liked to dance I would actually sweat as if I had a work out at the gym. That was when I saw Vanessa Bell Calloway and Lela Rochon in the mirror. Vanessa was watching us I guess like most of everyone. She was very nice and said something to me about it. We all heard a commotion and the next thing we knew Eddie had sent his body guards after me at the Lady's room door opening. We all looked a little surprised, so I went with them back to his table. I wasn't impressed, actually I was a little disappointed in Eddie by sending his body guards instead of doing it himself. They were his body guards not his servants. Eddie said that he was leaving and asked me for my phone number I wrote it down on a piece of paper. Then he asked if I'd go with him to have breakfast. That was a pretty standard request by any person you've might have met at a club. I didn't take it as some sort of "Booty Call". Even though Michael Bivens and Jeffrey were no where in sight and I wasn't sure how I was going to get home, I knew that I could hitch a ride with Micky or catch a cab. I wasn't even sure if I was going back to my apartment or back to Damian's place. I wasn't sure about nothing in my life or even what I wanted. However, I replied no thank you and then he said that he was leaving. I went back to Micky where we first stood and the next thing I knew is that Eddie walked over to me and handed me something. I looked down, and it was my phone number. Eddie has handed it back to me. Oh no, did I over play my hand? I wasn't playing a game. I just didn't think it was appropriate to leave with anyone that I just met no matter who he was. He and all of his entourage left and Micky looked at me like "what's next for you girl". Even Mickey knew most girls would have jumped at the opportunity. But I wasn't most girls, I was Debra grand daughter of GREAT MEN. Which made me conscious of how I represented my family. Lynn and Niecy were still there and I even ran into Michael Bivens, who was pissed at me for leaving him earlier at the front door of the club. I decided to go. I made my way to the door and the parking lot was crowded as well. I was looking around to see if there were any cabs. Then a limo pulled up and the window rolled down and it was Eddie. This time I got in…

When I noticed I was in a limo full of men I should have panache, but I didn't. I did get a little nervous when Eddie slipped off my thigh high boot. He was taking inventory, he really had a foot fetish. I guess I past the test because we drove off. We drove around for a few minuets looking for something open besides the usual IHOP. The one on Sunset was a little seedy that time of night. Besides everything else was closed. He asked if I were ok in going back to his house and he'd wake his cook to prepare something. I was a little reluctant but knew he had too much to loose to try something funny. His body guards Kenneth and Raymond all seemed to be regular guys and Eddie told me that they were HighSchool friends. We arrived at his rented home on Sunset Drive. I could tell since it was rented because it was decorated for the taste of a much "older person". He went to awake his cook, her name was Lisa and I asked to use the rest room. He directed me to a powder room right off the entry hall. This time I had to use it, when I was at the night club the bathroom was too crowded and since we were riding around to find a place to eat a lot of time had past. When I was in the powder room I noticed a phone and used it to make a call back home. I was a little reluctant because it was late and I didn't want to frighten my mother with a late night phone call. I wasn't concerned with the call showing up on Eddies bill but I thought he could effort a 5 minuet call to Pittsburgh. Besides he would have another number to contact me later should things go well in the future. I whispered to my mother hello and assured her that everything was ok and for her to guess where I was. Of course she had no clue and I replied "Eddie Murphy's house". Not too much ever surprised my mother when it came to me. I was always involved in something, not in a

bad way. She said that it wasn't good to be at mans house this time
of night and I assured her that I was fine and at least she now had
a number to trace should something would happen to me(there was
no *69 to call someone back). I told her that I loved her and would
not be staying long and I didn't. I hung up and went in search of
the kitchen. I could hear talking and followed Eddie's voice. He
did awake Lisa and she was another friend he grew up with. Very
friendly and didn't seem as if she were just awaken. Eddie was eating
a slice of cheery cake and offered me some with his fingers. I said
no thank you being I've never been much of a sweet eater. Come
to think of it, Lisa never prepared anything. Eddie took me to the
great room, you would have thought it was the middle of the day. I
know it had to have been around 3am. He took me by the hand and
we went upstairs to his room at the top of the stairs. We kissed and
talked for a while. He was rather quiet, not the jokester that maybe
one would think. I guess we had to get to know each other some
more. He did something that was kind of odd, he stood behind me
and put his face next to mine and said he wanted to see what we
looked like together. He actually looked for a while in the mirror at
our image together. Maybe he was concerned what we might have
looked like in paparazzi photo's. It reminded me of something girls
would do, like doodle a guys last name with their first name to see
how it may look and sound. I think most women have done that
before. There was so much traffic in his house for how late it was, I
guess this was something a rich handsome star would do in his free
time. There was a knock at the front door and some more people
stopped by. It was a woman. She was the sister of (Vanity), and
she had some friends with her. I could tell that she had been there
before and neither of us were concerned about the other. I could tell
she was a little taken back when she saw Eddie and I coming down
the steps. I said good night to Eddie and Kenneth rode me home. I
wasn't the type to stick around and see who would be the last man/
woman standing. My mother taught us not to be anywhere when the
lights came on…it was time to go. Besides it's only rewarding for me
when a man chases me!

I was hanging out way too much, and going into work
late much too often. This was an upstanding business I worked
for and I was blowing this opportunity. I had called Marc and he
wasn't around much and El answered the phone. He didn't know
that I was in LA and he asked if we could hang out. I thought it
would be a way for me to find out why Marc was not around much.
He agreed to meet me at my job for lunch. My co-workers were
surprise that I knew him enough for us to hang out. We just ate at
a sandwich spot near my job because of the amount of time I got
for lunch. I could tell he wanted more time and agreed to have El
come back to pick me up after work. He showed up when I got
off and we rode back to my and Cindy's apartment. I asked El how
Marc was and where he'd been hiding. He told me all about Marc
and his baby's mother, I was shocked..."Baby's mother", this wasn't
something that was common in that time. Now wonder he had been
so distant and unavailable. My feelings weren't hurt it just answered
all of the suspicion I had. El waited for a reaction from me to see
if would cry or fall into his arms. He put his arms around me like
I needed consoling and then tried to kiss me. I got angry that he
would try and test me and take advantage of me. What if I were
upset would he try to go in for the kill. I was turned off. Where was
his loyalty towards his brother? He'd probably figured that Marc
had any for me and I might have wanted revenge. I needed to get
us both out of my house before I would say something regrettable
to El. I might need him later to find out more about Marc and his
baby. I wasn't sure what more that I needed to know. I asked El
if he wanted to go past my cousin Damian's for a minute and he
would have done just about anything to stay in my company and
find out if I were angry enough to tell Marc. I wouldn't say a word.
I think most men will test their ability to conquer. I had sisters and
one of them always went behind my back and try to date anyone
who liked me. I know that it takes two. Damian was home and so
was Monique, she and I were always glad to see one another and
she saw El with me. I introduced them and she had sparks coming
from her eyes. Monique and I went in the bathroom for privacy, she

asked me what happened when I left there with Michael Bivens that night we went to the club "24 Karat". She said that he came back and talked about how jive I was when he had a hard time getting in. That I was all over the place with Eddie Murphy. We giggled and she said that she would have left his butt too. She asked was I with El and I told her not like that. I told her that I was seeing his brother Marc and things weren't good between us and El just came to hang out and check on me. She was glad to hear that I am sure. She had the green light to proceed. It took a while but they would eventually get married in 1995. She would send me an invitation.

Ms. Scofield would eventually sit me down for the talk... I knew it was coming. I was coming in late too often and I wasn't being responsible at work or home. Cindy was sick of me not having my half of the rent and was pretty patient with me for someone her age. I told Cindy that I understood and made arrangement to move out. I called my friend Lynn from Pittsburgh and she was excited for me to stay with she and Niecy, however she had to convince Niecy. What would I do no job and having to move all at the same time. I had no one to blame but myself. I was too young and had no direction and no adult supervision, and I needed some. Thank God Aunt Essie was a praying woman. Without her covering I might not have made it.

I was getting my things packed and ready to move and decided to do some laundry. We had to go outside and to the back of the building where it was kept. I only had maybe two loads to wash and walked outside barefoot like usual. Once I started my loads of laundry, I was returning to Cindy and my apartment I noticed a black SUV out front. I saw one of Eddie's body guards, Kenneth, at my apartment door and he said that Eddie wanted to see me and if I could come by now to see him. I told Kenneth that I was in the middle of doing my laundry (I never mentioned that I had to move) and was busy. He said that it would only take a minuet and that he'd bring me right back. I said let me grab my shoes and he said that it would only take a minuet and to come right now as I was and that he'd bring me right back home. I can't tell you why I never took the extra minuet to grab my shoes, I just got in the truck with Kenneth and we drove to Eddie's house.

It seemed as if there were always people around. Most of them worked for him and/or were friends that he grew up with. When I came in the front door Eddie was standing at the top of the steps and told me to come on up. I followed him into his bed room where he had tapes playing of the "Little Rascal's". I told him that I loved them as a child and watched them all the time growing up. Without notice or anything he walked over to me and started to kiss me. It was a little strange to me, it was without notice, but because he was so good at it I didn't stop him. This went on for most of the day. We stayed in his room and talked, kissed and watched tapes of the "Little Rascal's". I stayed the night. This went on for one more day and I kept telling him that I wanted to go home, that I needed a change of clothes and how I left laundry in the wash machine and my room mate was probably concerned where I was. However Cindy was probably used to me taking off. One of the reasons why she was in agreement that I should leave. I tried to call her a few times and couldn't catch her at home and I didn't know Lynn and Niecy's phone number to let them know that I would be delayed moving in with them. By the third day at Eddie's house we woke up and something happened that I thought I was ready for. We had sex. He was a great kisser however, it just seemed a bit odd to me. Nothing before seemed to lead into what was about to happen. I don't know what I expected…we just woke up and looked at each other and started to have sex. It wasn't what I expected since I had been there for a few days and nothing transpired. I just thought he was a little like me and wanted to check things out and see where I was coming from and what was my objective. Afterwards he had gotten a call to remind him that he had a meeting regarding the role he was playing in the up and coming movie "The Golden Child". We had taken a shower and he went into his walk-in closet to get dressed for his meeting. I had put back on my t-shirt and cut off jean shorts that Lisa has washed for me. Most of the time I was there I wore one of his shirts (which I was comfortable in). He put on a pair of black parachute pants with the zippers all over the legs, ankles, etc., and a Hawaiian looking shirt and a few gold chains. I asked him was he going on the set or to a meeting? And he replied...to a meeting, so I told him that I thought his outfit was a bit too much and that he should wear something more professional and take some of those chains off. That he looked like a "Drug Dealer" and he replied that I looked like the people that he sold the drugs too! We both cracked up laughing. I felt a mess being there without my own things and wearing his, but we never left the house. I was one of those girls who only liked dressing up when I had someplace special to go. It may have seemed that I was dressed up most of the time to people that are close to me only because I had jobs that required it, but when I am at home I am very casual. Eddie did change into what I suggested, a pair of slacks and dress shirt with just one gold chain. Eddie and I got into his car. I remember it was a convertible "Bentley" or something of that make. He rode me home and again we laughed that I had no shoes on. I just laid back in the passenger seat and let the wind blow through my hair with my feet up on the dash. He laughed again but I remembered he had a foot fetish...

CHAPTER EIGHT

Cindy had taken my things from out of the washer and I called Lynn when I returned home. No time like the present, so Cindy and I parted ways and it was very civil. We told each other that we'd miss each other and I got a ride from Micky to Lynn and Denise's apartment. It was in the "Wilshire" district, not as nice as "West Hollywood". My old building had only 4-6 apartments, the new one took up a half square block. The best thing about it is that the centre court yard contained a pool, which Lynn and Niecy never used before I got there. There were so many people who lived there. Many Mexican families with children and even a roster which crowed almost every morning. I got a kick out of it, I had a since of humor. Micky didn't stick around and Lynn met me at the door. She helped me carry my things up the steps and made some room for me in the walk-in closet we all shared. The apartment wasn't as nice as me and Cindy's. It was a lot smaller which never bothered Lynn and I. We all came from a group of three sisters, I however had an older brother. Lynn was very excited to have me there. She was bored during the days and wasn't employed at the time and Niecy was at work most of the day. We both knew that Niecy wasn't going to carry the weight of the two of us so we took the news paper, some baby oil and towels to the pool while we searched the "Want Ads" and got a tan. We both found something we thought we might like and would set up an interview, then walked to the store for some groceries. I was glad to have familiar associates from back home it gave me a sort of peace of mind. When Denise(Niecy) got home Lynn and I were cooking diner, something that they hadn't done much of since they'd move to California. She came home like a "sour puss" like most of the days. She was surprised to see me even though she was expecting me. She tried to change her attitude when she saw that I was there. She was glad to have diner and they had no table and chairs to sit at, so we sat on the mattress that Lynn and I would sleep on and Niecy stood at the counter in the kitchen and gave me the new rules and at the end of Niecy's speech she said that you two bitches better clean up the kitchen and get a job! Lynn and I both cracked up and assured

her that we were right on it. Niecy had a change of attitude when
she went in the closet and saw that I had a great wardrobe for her
to have access to for work. After she tried on a few items she went
to her evening ritual of looking for her boyfriend named "T". Lynn
would go with her. I stayed back and made a few phone calls, one to
my mother to let her know that I had moved into a new place with
two girls from back home and the other to my cousin Damian. I
was hoping that he would pass the information along to Aunt Essie
being I was still to chicken to call her myself. It had been months
since she'd heard from me and I was too embarrassed to call her
now. My last call was to El's house to give him my new number for
Marc, I was hoping that he would be there, however he wasn't. El
asked me what I was up to and wanted to see if he could come by.
I told him Friday would be good because I just moved and had two
roommate this time and wanted to clear it with them. He said ok
and that he would bring some friends with him and some drinks.
I said ok and gave him my new address, see you on Friday and we
hung up. I was hoping one of those friends he'd bring would be his
brother, Marc. It wasn't too long after Lynn and Niecy would come
home. Lynn was laughing so hard and told me what Niecy did. She
was spying on T and he had another girl at his house. Niecy had
climbed over something to get a better look at her and to bust T
on cheating. He heard them outside and tried to make Niecy leave
and she was making such a commotion outside his apartment. After
they tussled Niecy and Lynn left and come home. Niecy was made
as heck. I could hardly understand Lynn with all of her laughing
in-between her sentences. I thought it would be a good time to tell
them about my company on Friday. Nothing like getting over a bad
boyfriend with having a cute celebrity guest at your home. They
both screamed and Niecy was in the closet trying to figure out what
to wear even though we still had a few days before they'd be here.

   The next day Lynn and I sat out for our interviews. Mine
was with "Sport Connection" on Santa Monica Blvd in-between
"Hollywood" and BeverlyHills". Sports Connection was a up and

coming gym that all of the young artist worked out at. It was more complete then the usual gym. They had all kinds of different facilities one could utilize like massage, steam room, a juice bar and most exciting…roof top tanning where most people tanned in the nude.

I met with the manager named Joel. He was younger that what I'd expected and he hired me on the spot. I told him that I wouldn't be available to start until Monday. He was fine with that then showed me around and introduced me to everyone. Most of the employee's were around my age or in their late twenty's. They only thing that frightened me about my position is that we worked with computers and I hadn't any experience working directly with them as of yet. Joel said that they would train me and he wasn't concerned. Computers were new to the work force and most of his staff had to be trained on them. I caught the bus back home to my new spot with Lynn and Niecy. It was a much longer ride than when I lived with Cindy. Actually I had to ride past Cindy's stop and had to transfer to another bus that went cross town. When we all got home we shared about our day, both me and Lynn got the job which took some weight off of Niecy. She was still all smiles knowing she was one day closer to meeting El.

Well, Friday would finally come and I cleaned up the tiny efficiency apartment. It didn't take much since we were all very neat. I brought some snacks and fried some wing dings and played some music. Niecy and Lynn got home from work and right away Niecy started to primp for her evening with El. Some time had passed and I was getting concerned that maybe he wasn't coming. Not that it mattered so much for me but I knew how much Niecy seemed to be excited and I wanted to repay her for letting me stay. Most women wanted me to be their friend because of my association with celebrities. I didn't want her to be let down. Not that she didn't think that I knew him or not wasn't my concern, heck she and Lynn witnessed my meeting with Eddie Murphy. They both knew that was my MO. Finally our buzzer rang and I buzzed them in. I could see the anticipation of excitement on Niecy's face. Lynn was much cooler, she had dated "Dave Parker" of the "Pittsburgh Pirate's", so she was cool. I let them in and me and El hugged and I introduced them and El only brought one friend which made the balance off. He was in the industry but wasn't known to us. He played an instrument and worked with El on some music. They brought some beer and liquor. It started off a little stiff until everyone had a few drinks. We ate and played spades. It was a good night except for I was too afraid to ask about Marc. El must have thought I had forgotten about him by now and figured that he would now have a shot at dating me, or maybe just getting in my pants. We had a good time and El and his friend had to go, all of a sudden Niecy grabbed El around the ankles and said… "Don't go"! It caught El so off guard that he almost fell over and grabbed hold of the counter. I was so shocked and embarrassed, I could see that Lynn was surprised too. It was so awkward watching El peal back Niecy's arms from around his legs. It was such an uncomfortable situation for all of us, it came from out of the blue! When Niecy seemed to come to her senses she let go. El gave me a look like "Where did that come from?" He remained gracious and gave me a hug and said that he had a good time, he and his friend left. Lynn and I laughed about it later when we were in bed, I know we couldn't tease Niecy about it she didn't have much of a sense of humor when it came to herself.

That weekend I went to see Damian. He had company as usual, Monique and a new face was there named Kimberly. She wasn't alone, she had a friend with her named Whitney. Kimberly was dressed up and looked like a modern day "Flapper" of the 1920's. She wore a black fitted dress made of lace and wore her hair in finger waves with rhinestone jewelry, and bright red lipstick. Whitney wasn't as dressy. Monique wasn't feeling them and seemed to be glad that I came by. I was never fancy unless I had someplace to go that was a formal event. I said hi to everyone and Damian seemed not to care if I was there. He told me that Eddie had tried to date Kimberly as well. It seemed he was trying to start mess between the two of us from the door. I never cared what guys did behind the backs of women. He was young single and rich and most of all FAMOUS! I always did me until a man made it clear with a ring, then I would hold him accountable, until then I did me. By this time I'd already had two rings given to me and many more on the way. (Again the patterns). Monique and I sat on the couch watching Damian fawn all over Kimberly. She was from Minneapolis and looked like "Prince's crowd" the Revolution, pale skin with dark hair. She had a very out going personality and had us cracking up with her stories. Turned out she was under legal age and taken her older sisters ID before she came to California. Her real name was Rhonda and I wouldn't find that out until after we'd hang out a few times. She stayed at a number of motels. Because of her experience and body I thought she was much older. Kimberly was sort of built like a "Kim Kardashian". We wound up exchanging phone numbers and would later become friends.

On Monday I would go to work. Lynn would sometimes meet me there or after work so we could either use the facilities or ride the bus home. Sometimes we'd stop off and get something to eat.

There was a "Fat Burger's" around the corner which I learned to like. I wasn't much of a food eater before I came to Los Angeles. I learned to enjoy it in Cali, the food was always freshly prepared and much lighter than the food on the East Coast where it was mostly meat and potato type of meal.

Well, this particular day Lynn would stop in and I was just about to get off from work and we were going to use the steam room then retreat to the roof top for some sunning. She asked me if I knew this man who was staring at me and I replied he is always in here. She told me that his name was Jim Brown and he was a formal NFL player and now a "Movie Star". I hadn't a clue and didn't care. He was an old man to me and not my type.

I really didn't have a physical type then, I do now. Lynn knew everyone in sports. She always wanted to become a Sports Reporter and her grand father was a famous sports figure in history. He played for the "Homestead Braves", one of the first all black professional baseball teams. She could name every "Laker" where they went to school, what position they played, and what they averaged in a game.

We retreated to the roof to sun bath. Lynn wasn't shy about her body. There were a couple of older Caucasian ladies who were totally nude so Lynn decided to go topless, only not to have tan lines in her clothes when we went out. I on the other hand was a bit of a prude and not so comfortable with my body image, only because I always heard people call me skinny. I didn't know that my body was considered the best body type for a California movie star. I was shaped like a cross between "Rhianna and Zoe Saldana". Lynn was more of a "Jennifer Lopez" type with an athletic edge. Her arms and legs were more definably toned. And in the back of my mind I was always thinking of how God would think of me if I did anything He might see as out of line. I didn't know anything yet about grace and lived with a lot of condemnation. There wasn't anyone up there excepts us. I grew up in a C.O.G.I.C. environment and I had religion instead of relationship with Christ and didn't know that He had set me free, heck He came to set us all free! After Lynn and I walked to "Fat Burger's" to grab something to eat we caught the bus home. I was so happy to have her, someone I could be adventurous with. We would have many, one like the time Lynn Niecy , and a few of Niecys friends had all met up at this club in the Wilshire district, and Lynn and I rode with this white guy we'd just met and he kept us held up at his house because he was too drunk to drive us home. He stripped down to his red speedo's and went to sleep. We didn't know where we were. Thank goodness he did take us home when he got up the next day. Lynn always thought we would run into a "Charles Manson" type even though he was in jail. God watched over all of us.

One day will I was working at Sports Connection Jim Brown came in. I could tell that he was interested in me and he made me feel a little creepy at times. It wasn't him making the typical advances, I couldn't even put it to pen and paper to describe exactly what it was that he did...it just gave me the creeps. It was so lustful, like a hungry wolf circling his prey. He went and did his usual thing, and played racket ball. He always used the first room I think it was for him to be able to view me at my work station. He worked out most days so he had a chance to see me almost daily. When I got off Jim was sitting outside in his convertible Mercedes Benz at my bus stop. He had a big smile on his face. He asked me if I wanted a ride home, and told him, "heck no, I don't know you." He replied that I was safe because most of LA did know him. He also said it was day light, he was riding in a convertable, and everyone would see if he would try and do something to me. Meaning he couldn't kidnap me without having a lot of witnesses. I still said no thank you and got out of debating about it by my bus showing up. I got on the bus and rode to my next stop, where had to wait for the cross-town bus. When I got to my connection I noticed Jim sitting in his car parked on the corner, still smiling. He was waiting for my response and I didn't give him one. I simply waited for my connecting bus and got on. I watched outside to see if he was following my bus however I couldn't see. There wasn't a window on the back of the bus, just the sides of the bus. I got to my destination and crossed the street. I could see that Jim had made it there too. He drove along the side of me while I walked to my apartment. He kept talking to me as I walked. He said that I could have been home by now if I had taken the ride from him. I don't know why I didn't have the creeps still, this was a bit extreme, however, I was more intrigued by his persistence than thinking this was a little on the stalking side. I thought he just had patience being he was older and I must have sparked an interest in him. It was probably a little of all the above. When I got to my building he pulled over to the curb and asked me to stay a minuet and I told him he had enough of my time. And I wasn't to keen on him now knowing where I lived. The only thing is that our building was a little secure with gates and there were always a lot of people outside coming and going. Besides I didn't live a lone. When the girls got home I told them what happened and Niecy replied "That Moth'a F____r is crazy and don't full around with him he beats women! Well, I was like I had no intentions of seeing him, he was much too old for me and not my type. Lynn agreed but always the optimist, she said that those were rumors and we didn't know for sure but be careful. This went on for a few more times either he would be at my bus stop in the mornings or after I got off nevertheless I never got in his car. He played everything correctly, he tired different approaches and pulled back a bit so that I wouldn't find him creepy.

I hadn't seen my friend Wanda (from the accounting firm) in a while and I gave her a call to see how she was doing. I got her caught up to date in what I was up too and no longer worked at Elizabeth Arden and had moved from Cindy's. I knew Wanda wasn't much of a group person and if we were to hang out she'd rather it just be the two of us. She would pick me up in her two seater and we went to the first "Gay Pride" parade I had ever witnessed. It was exciting to me. I loved all of the creative costumes and floats and everyone was either drunk or just plain happy, either way they were having a blast and we were too. We sat on the hood of her car and took it all in. I saw one guy I met at Sports Connection. His name was Clem. He looked like a cross between Native American and something else, not quite sure of what, however, he was BEAUTIFUL! Clem's body was spray painted blue with sprinkles. He was dressed as a Unicorn. I would exchange numbers with him as well. He later got me a few modeling jobs. It was good meeting people in LA.

We had settled in nicely at Lynn and Niecy's apartment. We were always going out on the weekends and having a blast. One day while we were all squeezed into our small bathroom getting ready for another night out and I noticed something. Niecy and Lynn both got their periods and I hadn't. Most of the time when women

lived together somehow they'd sink up and have their periods all at
the same time. This would happened with me and my sisters. They
both looked at me with fear on their faces. I had noticed that I had
gained a few pounds not much but a few was a lot for me since
naturally I had a hard time gaining weight. Lynn thought it was
because of all of the "Fat Burger's" we were eating after work and
Niecy was like, "Naw, _itch your pregnant!" Terra rose upon my
face, oh my God! This was the thing that my mother Syreeta and
everyone else was trying to keep me from. How could I've let this
happen?! Lynn was the only rational one there, she told Niecy to
stop scaring me and asked me when was my last period. I couldn't
remember, I knew it was before the move. Well, I had been there of
more than a month, it was more like two or three. I never missed
my cycle and I instantly was terrified! However, we still went out.
All that night I couldn't enjoy myself I kept thinking what if I was
pregnant and how my life would end and how I would disappoint
everyone and oh my goodness what about Aunt Essie, she'd think I
was a heathen! I was a mess. When I went to work the next week I
couldn't function I kept worrying about my possible condition and
why was I in so much physical and emotional pain. I didn't know
much about pregnancy but I knew you weren't supposed to feel
pain until delivery, so why was I in so much pain.

Monday would come like it always did and I caught the bus
to work. I still had the pain coming from my female area. I knew
that my health insurance had not kicked in, however I needed to
see about myself. As fate would have it I passed out at work from
the pain. The next thing I knew I was being rushed to UCLA
Medical Center. My boss Joel called for the ambulance. They were
taking my vital signs and getting my personal information when I
heard a man's deep voice say that he was taking over and had me
transported to Cedars Sinai. Jim had taken over as if he were my
father or relative and no one questioned him. That was the first
time I recognized the power he had. He was making arrangements
for my treatment and everything. I was put in a private room and

was asked a mountain of questions that were very personal and I thought how could I answer them knowing that Jim was in the room with me. I didn't want him to know that I had slept with Eddie Murphy and that I might be pregnant or even something worst...Eddie might have given me something. Something had to have caused me the pain. I was still in pain.

I told the doctor that I might be pregnant and they would run a pregnancy test right away and to my surprise it came back negative...so what was the problem, now very frightened! They ran more test and gave me an ultra sound which showed that I had a fibroid tumor that was the size of an orange which blocked me from having my period and protruded my stomach because I was so small. That was what caused me all of the pain. Jim got me a specialist and I had the surgery to remove the fibroid. While I was in surgery Jim took the time to contact my mother. He must have gotten my contact information from my employer Joel. Jim had flown my mother to California right away. I had only been in the hospital for a few days when I heard my mothers voice in the hallway of the hospital. She sound upbeat and not concerned that I was in the hospital. She came into my room with a big smile on her face which I hadn't expected to see. I thought she would have a look of a little upset, instead she wore a smile. I was glad to see her. It had been two years since I've last seen any of my family back in Pittsburgh. My mother had already been in town for a day. Jim had picked her up from the airport and had brought both my mother and my room mate Lynn to his house until I got out of the hospital. I was upset with my mother she was acting as if she were on vacation. She was telling me how Jim picked her up from the airport and had taken her to his house and how nice he'd been and that she met his little girl, she was going on and on! Well, heck I thought...when did she get a chance to do all of that and why didn't she come straight to the hospital to see about me?! She said that I had just come from out of surgery and I was sleeping and wouldn't known if she was there or not. So Jim took her and my room mate Lynn to his home to make sure she was comfortable. In fact her took them to get something to eat and everything. She said that he was "The Hostess with the Mostess"! I thought what happened to the "Woman Beater" that everyone had warned me about?! The doctor came into my hospital room and gave me instructions on how to care for myself and that he thought I could be discharged the next day. I saw that Jim would follow my doctor into the hallway and they were talking privately. I couldn't hear what they were saying. I imagine it had to do with my discharged and after care. I knew that Jim even took care of my hospital bills. I was told not to lift anything over a certain weight and no chores of any kind, not too much standing until I got my strength back, and absolutely no intercourse. That was find by me, I figured that why I was in this predicament because of my sin. I thought because of my fornication I was being punished for my sin. Because I knew what the Bible taught…"the wages of sin is death"!

Jim suggested that I stay in his house until I recovered, however I heard my mother say that I should come home. Everyone was making decisions again for me and I knew that I wasn't ready to go back to Pittsburgh. Besides what would I do? I had come to California for my career in cosmetology and that wasn't going so good. I wasn't even working in my field and now this. Then Jim made a suggestion that Lynn move in with me so I'd be comfortable in his home. There was more than enough room. He had a 4 bedroom house with "Maid's quarters", a pool house with only he, his daughter Kimberly who was 3 years old at the time and a house keeper. Jim also had a pool man and Gardner to take care of the grounds so I had nothing to take care of but myself but because of how I was raised I knew to look out for Kimberly. She was only three and needed a mother figure and I didn't know why at the time that her mother wasn't in her life. Jim said that (Kimberly's) mother had a drug problem. I believe if she did, somehow it probably stemmed from the problems she had from Jim. I never saw Jim use anything but "Smirnoff Vodka", but his abuse could cause a person to not be their usual self! He assured me and my mother that this would be good for me until I figured what I wanted to do with my life while I recovered. They all seemed to have everything all figured out however I was still concerned...why was he doing all of this for me and what ever happened to all of the things they had said that Jim was?! They had seemed to forgotten what they had said about him and was being seduced by the glitz and the glamor! Was he being kind...or was he very calculating.

My mother stayed for a few more days. Jim took me and Lynn back to our apartment to get some of our things. He was so accommodating. He carried our things into his car and the only one who seemed to wonder what the heck was going on was Niecy. She still had her suspicions. She said that ya'll _itches were crazy and she was staying behind in our apartment. When we returned back to Jim's house he took my things up to one of the empty bed rooms where I wanted Lynn to stay with me. Even though there was another bedroom on the floor. For the next few days Jim took us every where, Venice Beach and out to diner and sometimes he even cooked for us. My mother would chip in. She had made herself quite comfortable there. He even took us to "The Playboy Mansion". That wasn't something I was comfortable with. I didn't like nudity. I had a preconceived opinion about people like that. They were sinners, but what was I? I hadn't discovered "Grace" as of yet and that we were all sinners before inviting Christ into our lives, but I had already done that as a child, so how come nothing had changed for me as of yet?! I was missing something... the renewing of the mind. We pulled up to a huge rod iron gate at the bottom of a very long winding driveway and Jim pushed the intercom, a voice answered and the gate opened and we proceeded to drive up. As we were approaching the top of the driveway I could see the Manson from a distance. We pulled up to the front of the door and Mr. Hefner was standing there in his infamous "Red Smoking Jacket" with a pair of slacks underneath. He looked like what I saw of him on television. He was welcoming and spoke to all of us. He mostly talked with my mother I guess because she was the first one at the door and she is very friendly. I could hear him welcome us and he briefly showed us around and offered us something to eat. There were always multiple chefs on staff at the mansion. I still wasn't much of an eater and would go with them into the dining room where there was a variety of assortments of pastries and deserts. The chef was accommodating as well, he came out of the kitchen and asked us specifically what we wanted to eat. Mr. Hefner's staff was something to experience. They were there to fulfill what ever any guest desired. There were a few other people I can't remember just how many but not much. Nothing like the pool parties that sometimes we'd get a little insight to on t.v. Jim would finish our tour around the grounds. He knew it well since he'd been there on numerous occasions. He took us to the infamous "Grotto"! It was a man made cavern with a hot spring type of indoor hot tub. It had lights that came from inside the hot tub and seating along the inside of the water. Jim said that we could get in if we wanted too, however I knew that we didn't come equipped with swimming suits neither would it be wise for me to get in community water after my surgery, which was a good excuse for me. I didn't want Jim to see my body. I knew that he wanted me in that capacity and I didn't want to lead him on. It felt a little creepy to me that a man of that age difference desired me in a sexual way. However, it didn't stop my mother and Lynn from getting in regardless of not having swim suits and they stripped down to their underwear and got in. You couldn't see them totally nude or anything, however I could see the silhouette of their bodies from in hot tub lighting. My mother had the attitude of "in Rome do as the Romans do." I on the other hand was very uncomfortable with her decision to get almost naked in front of a man whom we hardly knew and had a thing for me. I wanted for her to display the morals of a mother who trained me to value myself and not to freely give of myself to a man who wasn't my husband. I wanted for her to portray a God fearing woman with morals, however, she wanted to be free of always having the responsibility of being a mother. She knew that we were all now young adults except for my baby sister Holly who was back in Pittsburgh. With her knowing that, I guess that was why she let her hair down.

Jim saw the look of disappointment and disgust on my face and tried to comfort me by saying that he's seen everything before and she needed to have a good time. Still it didn't take the felling of shame away I felt about her actions. What he saw her do I thought he would expect the same things from me since she had raised me. I didn't want him to think that I was easy or wasn't raised without a moral compass. After a few hours there we returned to Jim's house. Everyone was not ready to go to sleep except for me. I only stayed up because of I was the common denominator between everyone. I was tired and my body was still not fully up to capacity after my surgery. Jim would put on some music like he always did. We both had that in common however we didn't have the same taste in music. He loved Billy Ocean song "In the Love Zone" and wore a song out titled "Pop Pop Pop goes my mind" by Gerald LeVert. Til this very day whenever I hear those songs, they remind me of the day's with Jim. Not in a bad way, just reminds me of those times. This time Jim made sure he gave them swimsuits to put on. I sat on the edge of his pool while watching them all swim and frolic. He had made them drinks and everyone seemed to be having a good time, however I couldn't join in. I was tired and couldn't go into the pool. Afterwards we would retire to his living room. Jim sat on his sofa in the corner seat which was his favorite spot on his sofa. It gave him a complete view of the living room and outdoor space which was something I learned from my father (was not to sit with your back to the door so you can see any on coming trouble). My mother sat beside him on the sofa, Lynn on an adjacent ottoman and I sat on the floor. Mostly because I really wanted to be in a bed. At sometime during the conversation and I can't even tell you just what we were even discussing my mother pushed up on Jim in front of Lynn and I. Jim had a look of shock on his face and immediately pushed her away so fast and because of her drinking and being a small woman, she flew to the floor. He wasn't trying to hurt her or her feelings, it was just a quick reaction, and at the same time he bolted out "I don't want you I want your daughter"! Everyone was so uncomfortable at this very moment. He was helping my mother up when Lynn and I sat there frozen. I believe it was a combination of my mothers drinking which also lead to her falling and not that Jim shoved her hard. I couldn't take anymore embarrassment that day and Jim told me that I could lay across his bed and get some rest. On my way to his room Lynn met me in the hall way and said that she was sorry for me and she was embarrassed for the whole thing of my mothers behavior. I just wanted to pretend that it never happened and go to sleep hoping that know one would notice...however we all did. Jim was upset that he thought he may have blown his chances with me because of making my mother fall off of the sofa to the floor. However I understood the entire thing and was simply embarrassed for everyone. I could see why my mother could have mistaken Jim's kindness for in tress in her, besides, they were closer in age than he and I. They'd spent a great deal of time together while I was in the hospital and he had sent for her and welcomed her in his home. And for the most part they had things in common being she was closer to his age. I just wanted to go to sleep and when I would wake up it all would have been some sort of bad dream.

I slept hard. It was the first time that I had slept in a real bed since I left my mothers house, except at Eddies. I slept on top of the covers not to get too comfortable in Jim's bed. He had gone back into the living room to get my mother and Lynn back in a comfort zone and to assure them that things were perfectly all right. They must have both turned in after I fell asleep. I noticed it got quiet and felt uncomfortable in my spirit. I woke up and saw that Jim was sitting on the floor at the bottom of his bed watching me sleep or staring up my sun dress that I had on. He could see that he was caught and I startled him by waking up and catching him in that position. He stated that he didn't want to wake me and said that he was only checking up on me. I let that be his excuse and he left the room and I fell back to sleep. Even though it felt weird I wasn't too uncomfortable knowing that my mother and Lynn were somewhere in the house. So it made it easier for me to fall back asleep (being that I was still on medication) but mostly I was very tired from all of the drama.

The next day Jim was trying to smooth things over. Up to this point he hadn't done anything wrong! Well, at least nothing that I could prove. I couldn't read his intent. He took us out one more time before my mother had to leave and, secretly, I wanted for her to go. She finally got in contact with Syreeta and she would come over to Jim's house to see us. Mommy had explained everything to her how we wound up at Jim's house and that I had surgery. Syreeta wasn't the suspicious type and if she'd thought anything she kept it to herself. Jim was taking us to a night club called "El Bravado's". I had been there before with Eddie. This time Lynn called our old room mate Niecy to see if she wanted to join us. Lynn must have convinced her that Jim wasn't the bad person that they heard about. That we were actually were having fun and that she was missing out. So the next thing I knew Niecy showed up at Jim's dressed and ready to hang out with us. My mother would stay back this time with Syreeta which made me happy. I didn't want to see if she do anything else to embarrass me. They were all waiting for me to finish getting ready and when I came out my mother made a comment on my dress. I might have been a bit risky for the time, however not for todays society. It was a fitted black stretch cotton knit mini not to high and long sleeve. But this is where it got a little sketchy...it was off the shoulders and had cut outs on the sides which were the top and bottom of the dress was held together with two round metal rings like the dress "Julia Roberts" wore in the movie "Pretty Woman", except my dress was all black. I even had my hair wild and curly like hers even though the movie hadn't come out as of yet, it was strictly my own creation. I had that talent which made me good at my craft making women over. I

enjoyed it. My mother thought it was too revealing and I thought
she had a lot of nerve after the playboy mansion ordeal. At least I
had clothes on I thought! Syreeta was always the voice of reason.
She said that I looked cute and let her wear the dress while I had
the window of youth to pull it off. So Jim Lynn and myself got
into Jim's convertible Mercedes and Niecy rode with some friends
she had invited. When we arrived we immediately got through the
crowd of people waiting in line. That was the nice thing of dating
celebrities...NO LINES! We were escorted to the back of the club
to the "Velvet Rope" section for VIP's. We were seated in the back
which had a view of the dance floor. Jim ordered for us and Niecy
came with us and her friends stayed in the common area. After
we'd been there for about 15 minuets Niecy said "Oh no there is
going to be trouble"! There was Eddie and has entourage at the
velvet rope trying to get seated and the only available seats were at
our table which he didn't want since he had spotted me there with
Jim and besides the last time we saw each other it wasn't on good
terms. After which seemed to be about 10 minuets Eddie finally sat
down at the only available table in the VIP...our table. The only
people who seemed to be ok were Jim and myself. Jim didn't seem
to be bothered, I believe because Jim was the oldest and probably
most mature or at least I thought. Also because Jim knew I didn't
care what Eddie thought. I was with a new man who was showing
me that he cared about me. Jim had opened his home and wallet
up to my family, friends and myself so far without a motive except
to make sure I was healing! Eddie had leaned in to talk to Jim and
later that evening Jim told me what the conversation was about.
Eddie had told him that I was trying to set him up and extort him
saying that I was pregnant. Since Jim was with me every step of the
way with my medical care he knew the truth and that I had fibroids
and it not only blocked my period, it made my stomach protrude.
Jim took into consideration that I was young inexperienced and
frightened. Then Jim stuck up for me, he told Eddie that I had
a medical condition and wasn't trying to extort him and if he'd
talked to me and manned up that he could have found that out

for himself, and for him not to worry about anything concerning me that I was now his woman. It was a very tense moment for everyone around including the bouncers at El Bravado's and Eddies. Jim didn't roll with an entourage, he was his own man. This was one of many things that Jim would do to make me fall hard for him. He was becoming the person that I needed. He was my protector, friend, care taker and later lover. He had the patients of a mature man that would beat out anything a younger man of much less experience had to offer. Eddie didn't want to hear what Jim had to say nevertheless he wasn't going to budge and sat there uncomfortable the rest of the evening, however Jim and my friends stayed and partied. When we returned back to Jim's house the girls couldn't wait to tell my mother and Syreeta what happened and Syreeta replied...it was the dress!

CHAPTER NINE

My mom left and went back home to Pittsburgh. By this time people were hearing about me and my life in Cali. All kinds of rumors were circulating. Funny how things could travel without social media. Everyone Lynn and I were friends with or associated with were trying to get on board. They were even contacting Niecy as well wanting to come out for a visit. Lynn friend Sherrie and Niecy's sister Lisa were first of many who came to visit. Jim never seemed to mind when people showed up. I believe he thought it gave him more insight to who I was, but that wasn't true. I hadn't any real friends yet, some who were cool with me back home from High School like Belinda Carter, Michelle Moore and Nancy Johnson aka Bunny. They were my childhood friends who shared small secrets and went to dances with and sometimes even got bullied together. Everyone that I had around me were new associates and later would become friends of mine, well not all of them.

My first family visitor after my mother was my brother Stanley. I hadn't seen him for a few years. He left home and joined the army and was stationed in Germany. I was very happy to see him and he was too, however my brother was a little older than me and knew of the rumors about Jim being an abusive man. He was more observant for the most part and was enjoying the parties that Jim would impromptu give. They would just seem to happen. All you need is the beautiful weather of LA and a pool and wala'... you had a party! This one in particular had a lot of things going on that I wasn't aware of. There were a few celebrity sightings like TK Carter and Whitney Houston's brother Gary. I kept wondering why people kept disappearing, they were going to the pool house to get high. There was a steam room in the pool house that they were using to smoke in. Everything from "Free Base" to "Pot" and because they were in the steam room I never smelled it. I was very green. I wouldn't have known the smell of too much of anything. California was the first time for me to see anything. Even while I attended college most of the parties only served some form of alcohol.

I was so happy that day and it was the first time that I was able to get in the pool after my surgery. Jim kept me preoccupied with a little PDA. We sat on the pool step and it was one of the first kisses I shared with him. I was getting quite comfortable with him. I was still at this time sharing a room with Lynn upstairs. I felt so secure on his lap. Jim had the body of a Greek god. He made me feel safe. I was authentically myself for the first time. Not having to live up to what others thought. Jim was making me fall for him.

My brother said that T.K. was going to show him around and they and some other people had left. The party would wound down and soon it was just Jim and I. That was the first time that I would sleep in the bed with him. No sex just intimacy. He held me we talked and went to sleep. He probably knew that I wasn't ready for anything else. I had just got comfortable with the age difference and no longer saw it as weird. I was afraid because of my surgery and felt a little uncomfortable with my brothers opinion of me being with someone much older, besides I wasn't experienced much and was religious and wanted to honor the "Commandments" even though I didn't earlier. I thought that was my problem and why I had a problem with Eddie. I had committed fornication, and my price for that was the fibroids and surgery and I didn't want to pay any more penalties for not obeying God! And if anyone could understand that would be Jim being he seemed to know more than any man I'd dated before.

My brother never came back the next day and I was concerned. Jim wasn't concerned but didn't want to share with me why. He knew why and knew the signs. My brother was on drugs, and people who are addicted go where the drugs are. He would surface soon and Jim tried to make arrangements to take him to the "Playboy Mansion", however, that was a no no for Mr. Hefner. You could invite as many women to the Mansion, however only Mr. Hefner could invite the men. Those were his rules. So Jim would make other plans for Stanley's last day of his visitation. He suggested that we go to El Bravado's again. This time it was Jim, myself, Stanley Lynn and Wanda(my friend from the accounting firm). Niecy and her friends went in a separate car. Jim was irritated because of an earlier comment I made about a girl named LaVaticia who invited herself to the pool party and brought Jim a gift. It was a gold chain. When she placed it around his neck he immediately took it off of himself and placed it around my neck in front of her. Then she left. Jim though I had forgotten all about the incident but I hadn't and brought it up before we left the house. My timing was not good. That was my first experience with his abuse…he slapped me and Lynn heard it. He said to me that I shouldn't let anyone get in between us and that no matter what a woman does it didn't reflect him. And that he showed her who he wanted by placing the neckless around my neck. Lynn came into the hallway and asked me if he'd just hit me. I barely answered her, I was in shock. He somehow made me feel as if I had caused him to hit me. That's how convincing most abusers are. When we arrived at the club we were escorted to the VIP. I could only imagine that the managers were hoping not to have another incident. Well, luck wouldn't have it. Everyone was ordering drinks and Stanley was dancing with all of these pretty girls and my friend Lynn. Lynn was very pretty too. She was my brothers flavor but I am sure that he didn't come all of this way to meet someone from home and besides Lynn had someone she was in love with back home named Otis. No one seemed to notice that I was upset, they were all doing their own thing. Jim kept a close eye on me and the only time that I moved was to go with him. I saw my brother talking to some older man for a minuet and then my brother came over to me and said…"That's Ron O'Neal" and I was like so, and my brother said he is the man who played "Super Fly" and again because of my age I didn't know or even care much about who people were in Hollywood. Especially if they were before my time. I respected the movie and that it was very popular, I couldn't appreciate the Black Exploitation era movies. I wasn't an adult when those movies were made to identify with them. However, I do now! My brother said that Mr. O'Neal asked him if I was with him and my brother told Mr. O'Neal that he was my brother. He never told Mr. O'Neal that I was with Jim and Mr. O'Neal never thought that either or he wouldn't have grabbed my hand when I walked by. He was trying to talk to me and I wanted to be nice but knew that if I spoke to him longer than a few seconds it might set Jim off...and it did. It was such a big commotion that we were all escorted out of there and this time asked not to come back. Stanley and Jim were arguing and I was so confused to what happened? Jim Lynn Wanda and I got in Jim's car and drove home so fast driving like a mad man up Sunset Plaza Drive. My brother got in the other car with Niecy(Denise) and her friends. When we all arrived at the house the mess hit the fan. My brother stood toe to toe with Jim. Everyone was getting in between the two of them, and then Jim backed off. If he hadn't I don't know what would have happened and who might have won. I didn't want for my brother to get hurt. I was screaming at Jim and threatened to leave. My brother wanted me to and beg me to go back home with him. I wasn't ready to leave Jim or California yet. I don't know why I couldn't see the signs. I blamed the drinking and all of these different personalities anything but the truth of it! Jim was controlling and I wasn't ready to throw in the towel! My brother knew if this would happen simply because of getting the attention of a man, what would happen to me if I were with Jim by myself with no witness!? Super Fly started a Super Fight, or so I thought!

I hadn't witnessed my brother cry since we were children. He cried for me, that I wouldn't leave with him the next day. I can't explain in words why I wouldn't leave with my brother. I didn't want him to cause him worry. It wasn't that I was afraid for my future back home, or even my future there with Jim. I had a destiny to fulfill and somehow I knew this part of my journey and it wasn't over and I was going to learn something valuable and I wasn't going to die in it! Jim called a cab to take Stanley to the airport and as much as I could I tried to assure him that I was where I wanted to be. Stanley just excepted my decision to stay and took the flight home back

to Pittsburgh. Jim would soon try to make things right. I started
to travel with Jim on business occasions. He would do lectures or
appearances for different organizations. When we would travel I
could see the strange looks we would get from people at times.
Sometimes people just simply thought that I was his daughter until
he may have given me a look of love between a man and woman,
or other times he might hold me not like a parents and then we
would get a look. Other times people would simply say something in
reference to him being my father and that was when Jim might speak
up. The only time I can recall this happening in California was at
Venice beach with my mother and Lynn. People thought my mother
was Jim's wife and Lynn and I were their daughters. Mostly people
in California were used to seeing couples who were much different
in age. It was common place for a man to have a much younger wife.
Because Jim wasn't concerned with the opinions of others neither
was I and besides he would handle anyone who he thought might
have insulted me in any shape or form.

This time I was meeting more of Jim's friends and business
associates. We would have lunch or diner with people like Don
Cornelius or Barry Gordy. And even having OJ and Nicole Simpson
over for lunch. Funny thing OJ never remembered meeting me
prior to them coming to lunch at our house. We briefly met at my
old job Elizabeth Arden when he came in to purchase somethings
and he disregarded me having knowledge of the product and
looked for someone whom he thought might have been more
qualified in his eyes. He looked at me as if I were just "the help"!
I never brought it up only to Jim a little later after they left. We
would have diner a few times more over the years Jim and I were
together, however O.J. and Jim only had two things in common,
abusing women and having played football.

Don was a bit of a shock to me for various reasons. One
he had great taste! I loved his home. It sat on the back end of the
caverns. It wasn't grand or ornate. It had more of a modern day

cabin feel. The beams were white washed and he had a lot of off white over stuffed furniture and lamb skinned rugs. He had a stone fire place that went from ceiling to floor. He owned a lot of "Alaskan Husky's" and they roamed freely through the house. They almost looked like part of the decor. However I didn't view him as the "Soul Man" that I grew up watching on Soul Train! He was an elegant man. The thing that I was taken back about the most is that he had a white spouse. She however was very beautiful. Tall, blonde and looked like a fashion model(more like a young Yolanda Foster). Let me clear that up. I can't remember if they were married or not, however, it was unexpected for me that so many men of esteem once they hit a certain plato, they mostly had white partners. Jim would never take that as an option. He was very proud and attracted to his women. He once shared with me why would I work to make money in order to give it right back to the white community by marrying a white woman. Jim also said that most black women wasn't afforded the opportunities that white women had and that he wouldn't add to that. Mr. Cornelius was still very pro-black in his efforts to make sure black people had a voice in "Hollywood". He put his time and money behind his vision. A class act, Mr. Gordy as well. There is a reason for peoples success at those levels. They are much different from ordinary folks. They aren't box thinkers and aren't afraid to make things happen. Mr. Gordy was one of them. But what most don't have the opportunity to know is that he too was very gracious and humble. He live in a home which looked like a castle and it was very ornate, however very tastefully decorated. He had wrought iron glass 20-25 foot french doors which lead out to a beautiful garden where he Jim and I along with Gordy's girlfriend at the time and now wife Gracie. Again I was taken back, not because of her being a white woman but because I didn't find her attractive in comparison to him to have dated "Diana Ross"! She was very thin but curvy. She was brunette with very long straight hair and a little washed out looking. She was quiet and had a few cats which she attended to a lot while we were there. She didn't say much while we had lunch. Mr. Gordy seemed to like me or maybe that was just his personality. He was very engaging, made you feel valuable, and wanted to incorporate you into the conversation. He was very kind. The lunch was very good. I remember we had collard greens without them seasoned with pork and they were good. I told Mr. Gordy that was how my mother taught me to make them. After lunch Jim and Mr. Gordy played a little tennis and Gracie and I watched from the side lines. Those were many of the experience that I had with Jim and his peers which solidified our relationship for me. He was proud to have me in his life and on his arm. I was spending a lot of quality time with Jim and less of my friends.

Lynn's boyfriend back in Pittsburgh had decided to come out and see what all of the ruckus was. He never liked missing out on a good time. So Otis was next to come out to visit. However he didn't stay at Jim's house. Otis too was his own man and a bit older than Lynn, so he stayed at a hotel. However he did come over to visit for drinks and conversation. He and Lynn had gotten engaged and were going back to Pittsburgh, not before Jim would take Lynn Wanda and I to "Magic Johnson" big 25th Birthday Bash held at a hotel. Otis made sure he didn't loose Lynn to a celebrity or sports figure. She was a knock out. I was going to miss her.

Now the only ones left in the house were Jim myself our house keeper Gloria(who I hired) and Jim's daughter Kimberly who was 3 years of age.

Jim had an up and coming event that would be one of the "High Lights" of his life and career. He was being inducted into the "NFL HALL OF FAME"! This was and is a huge honor, and I would go with him to Canton, Ohio to witness it first hand with Jim. Since I came from a big spots town, I knew this was something BIG! From the moment we touched down in Canton it was fan fare! There was as much paparazzi and fans at the airport then in Los Angeles. We had handlers who whisked us away by limo to the hotel were we would be staying. The entire weekend would be full of planned events. It was a whorl wind of events. First starting with the event planner who gave Jim his itinerary and took us to diner where they had a meet and greet. I was being shuffled around through the sea of people and press. Again most thought I was his daughter. I was never offended by it. I thought it was to be expected by having such an age difference and besides Jim always handled it by speaking up and correcting them. He must have sign autographs for an hour. We did managed to get back to our hotel room. He was elated and it was great to see him having fun and it was all about him for a change. I was happy for him. Before this it was all about me and getting me well and putting up with all of the traffic that was coming and going in our house. We made love and turned in early we had a full day ahead of us. We were up very early the next morning and were getting our updates from one of the planners. Our first event was the Hall of Fame brunch. There were so many speakers and guest speakers and then Jim got up to say a few words. It was very brief he wanted to save his speech for the field. He took photo's with invited guest and made sure that I was included. He would correct any paparazzi should they not want me in the photo's. He even told them that I was his fiancé, even though I didn't have a ring on my finger and that was probably why I wasn't recognized as Jim's woman by some people.

The next stop was to a football field and boy was it hot. I didn't expect it to be so. Since I was from that area I knew the weather could have been anything but! The speeches seemed like it would go on for hours, but I was so proud of him it didn't matter. We got whisked off again to the parade where Jim and I rode on the back of a convertible. The crowd was cheering and there was a huge turn out. That was the moment when I learned just how much he was respected in his field. I was happy to share that moment with him and will never forget it. I was proud that he was my man as well! We would got off to another event back at the hotel, but Jim called it short and we went back to our room, but not before he had made arrangements with a local to take us out later. Jim always liked to hang out with the locals no matter where we travelled. We needed the nap. Between the heat and all of those meet and greets, and excitement, it was a full days work. My cheeks hurt from smiling so much. We got up and got casually dressed and the driver took us to a local spot where locals hung out. It reminded me of Pittsburgh. Nothing fancy just good music, good food and good fun. They had a really good DJ and you could tell that the owner had a heads up that we were coming. He had a small section in the back of the club roped off for us. People were surprised that Jim didn't travel with body guards. He didn't need any. Very few men would challenge him in anyway. I never saw one. It felt good to be with people who we could just be ourselves with, or so I thought. The owner kept asking us if we needed anything and Jim ordered his favorite vodka and some sort of fruit juice. I would order the same knowing that I would never finished it and it was something he liked and would finish mine. Jim had no idea just how much I loved him and enjoyed seeing him being honored. The owner asked if Jim could sign a few autographs for him and Jim did reluctantly. He knew once he started it would be difficult stopping. Then this larger built woman came sash shying across the room and disregarded that I was even sitting there. This was one of the first blaytin disrespectful experiences that I had with a fan or woman. She looked me dead in my eyes as if she were saying to me "Watch a real woman work" and sat down on Jim's lap and without notice Jim shoved her off of his lap and she fell to the floor. Everyone had a look of surprise like "What happened"?! No one came to her rescue. She wasn't hurt in the least, but the owner ran to Jim to see if he was ok and apologized to him for any disrespect. She picked herself up off of the floor and Jim wasn't done. He told that woman "Don't you see me with my woman"! "Did I invite you to my lap"! "Don't you ever disrespect me and my woman again"! Well, if that wasn't clear, now it was. Even to me I would never worried about any woman coming between Jim and I ...EVER!!! I don't know if she voluntarily left but I didn't see her the rest of the night. All in all it was a great time and event. We would go back to Los Angeles the next day. It felt good to be home. I was now calling Jim's house home. The reason for not calling it home is that he had lived there since 1968 and I was just a baby at that time. He had lived there as long as I had been alive.

Not too long after we got home from the Hall Of Fame, Jim and I went to Sports Connection, he loved to stay in shape. His favorite thing to do was to play racket ball. I would go with him. I had no need to work out, I was naturally thin. It was good to see some of my old co-workers and boss. I watched Jim through the plexi glass while he played, when a gentleman named Richard Lawson walked in. He was an up and coming actor and had just landed the role of Diane Carol's lover on the popular show "Dynasty". He was so elated that he went through the crowd hugging and kissing everyone. It was a great role to land for the time. When he got to me, he kissed me too in celebration, and Jim saw it from inside the plexiglass. I pretended to be happy for him which I was however, the look on Jim's face let me know that there was going to be a problem. When we left I waited for some sort of questioning and thought that I had escaped an argument, so we just went home.

We carried out the rest of our day. After diner Jim was a little playful and wanted to play hide and seek with his daughter Kimberly. So we did. Things got a little weird when Jim turned off the power to the house while Kimberly and I hid together. She was much to young to hide alone. She and I hid upstairs and every time Jim seemed to get near us we'd escape and find another spot. I seemed dark and very eerie and I could see that Kimberly was getting frightened. So I asked Jim to stop. He had been drinking since we got home from the gym. He turned the power back on and Niecy and now Doreen who were both now staying there came up from the pool house and asked what was going on because the power was out. We told them we had been playing hide and seek with Kimberly or (Kimbo) which Jim sometimes called her. They hung out with Jim and I for a few minuets and went back down stairs to the pool house and I put Kimberly to bed. Jim fixed himself another drink and made me one too. I didn't want one. I really didn't drink much but took it anyhow just not to make him angry. He was behaving very strangely and I was going to keep quiet until I knew what it was. He was sitting in his usual spot on the couch and I was sitting on the floor adjacent from him.

Then it happened, Jim asked me in the most intimidating voice..."Why did you let that nigga kiss you"?! I just froze! I couldn't think of just what he was talking about and who are you talking to in that manner?! Before I knew it Jim had threw his drink in my face and said at the same time..."Don't play crazy with me"! I wasn't playing crazy I just couldn't think of what he was referring to or about. We had an entire day pass and usually they were full and before I knew it he grabbed me by my hair and dragged me into his bedroom, all while I was screaming punching and kicking trying to get him to let me go! When we reached the door frame I was holding on to it trying not for him to get me inside. I had forgotten that Kimberly was in ear shot of us. She had to have heard it all, but either was too afraid of knowing what to do she stayed in her bed room. Because the maids quarters was in the other side of the house it was very possible that Gloria might not have heard it. Since he was much stronger than I was he got me inside the bed room and locked the door. When he locked the door I managed to escape his grip. He didn't go directly after me since he knew that I was trapped inside. I ran towards his closet and reached inside his fur coat pocket where he kept his gun and pulled it out. He taunted me because I was shaking so much. He launched at me and I pulled the trigger. I flew back on the bed and he smiled and laughed. He said you would really kill me and he lunged at me again, this time I fired and because I was laying on the bed the bullet went up into the ceiling and Jim unlocked the bedroom door and ran out of the front door into the night. I locked myself in the bed room and called the police and held onto that gun for dare life! That was when there was a frantic knock on the bedroom door. I thought it was Jim. I knew it couldn't be the police that fast. It was Doreen she heard the gun fire and wanted to know what was going on. When she saw me she knew something had happened because I was in a disarray. I had been crying and my hair was all over the place and I was breathing heavily and visibly still shaking. I told her that Jim had just beat me and I shot at him to get him off of me. I knew he wasn't hit because there wasn't any blood anywhere. I told her that I called the police and that they were on their way. She asked me where was Jim and I replied that he ran outside. So she said lets get out of this room before he comes back and so she held on to my arm and I heard onto the gun as we walked slowly outside and up the curved driveway which was very dark… when I heard "Drop that weapon"! That's when I thought…"What weapon"?! The next thing I knew Doreen and I were surrounded by the LAPD. One of them came over to me and slowly removed the gun from my hand and put his arms around me. He knew that I was in shock and walked me down the curved driveway. I felt like I was outside of myself. Like I was watching a movie of all of this. They were like a swat team I might have seen in a movie! Helicopters, flash lights, and about 4 police officers had Jim face down on the ground with only his terry pool wrap on. I was still in the arm of the police officer when I heard Jim yell out to me "Debra tell them that this was all a big mistake"! I was thinking how dare he ask this of me! He just beat me and I was terrified and angry at the fact that I didn't do anything and it would be a while even before I'd learn of what he was even angry about. It didn't matter what he was angry about, it was no excuse for any man to beat a woman and beside my father always told me to never allow a man to do that to me. I had never witnessed anything like that before, not with me or anyone in my family.

I was taken inside and there was so much going on inside. Police were all over the house. Some were talking to Gloria the house keeper, others were questioning Doreen and Denise who stayed upstairs the entire time. They were taking everyones statements and took me to Cedar Sinai Hospital. There were so many reporters outside in the hallways of the hospital and after the doctor treated me, not much they could do for cuts and bruises. A group of police and detectives took pictures of my injuries and moved everyone out of the room. One of the detectives told me that they have been trying to get charges to stick on Jim for years and that they would provide me with attorney given by the state should I corporate. They made me many promises like getting his house and Jim's money. I was confused...to what did him beating me have to do with all of that?! I never asked for any of that and I wasn't sure what to do, this never happened to me before. I just wanted out of there and didn't even have a plan where I should or could go. All of my associates were living with Jim and I. I was too embarrassed to call Aunt Essie, it had been more than two years since I've seen her and now that I was in trouble I was too embarrassed to contact her now! I just wanted to go, but I didn't know just where. I knew that God always gives us a door to escape, however I was even to embarrassed to seek Him. Today I know that is Who I would call on first.

The detective took me back to Jim's house and told me since it was a domestic that I could stay at the house. I did not want to stay there. That was Jim's house and I didn't want any reminder of what had just taken place. So the detective gave me his business card and let me get some of my things and I drove off in my Suzuki Jeep. When I got to the top of the driveway there was a sea of reporter, news stations of all kinds. Even a helicopter driving over head and I managed to drive threw them and drove around until I stopped at a motel in Hollywood. I parked around the back and got checked in. I hadn't told anyone where I was going, I didn't know where I was going. After I got checked in I took my key and went to my room. I turned on the tv and sat there on the bed to collect my thoughts, then I heard the phone ring...who could it be I thought. No one even knew I was there. When I answered it I recognized the voice, it was Jim's best friend George Hugely who was the head chief of police of investigation of fraud. He asked me if I was ok and that he wanted me to come to his house where Jim was for us to talk. I couldn't think of how he knew how to find me without todays technology which prove it's been around for a very long time. Or knowing Jim he might have put a tracking device on my car since I found a tape recorder of his in his office next to our bed room, where he had been recording my phone calls when he was away. It wasn't long before George was at the door of my motel room. He gathered my few things and we got in his truck, and left my truck parked at the motel. I had never been to Georges house prior to this. He carried my bag inside and there on the sofa sat Jim. He waited for my response before he said anything. I didn't say thing. George brought his wife in the living room with us so I might be comfortable with a woman being there. None of that mattered to me. I was thinking how in the heck did Jim get out of jail so fast and who would allow him to be in the same room with me right after the beating occurred. Jim and I sat on opposite ends of the sofa while George and his wife sat in twin chairs to sort of mediate the conversation. George started out as if he were so concerned for my well being and asked me how I was feeling. He was doing damage control and was very good at it. Heck I was a young woman and was in the room with Jim with 2 degrees in Psychiatry from Syracuse University and the head of fraud of police, which I know took a great deal of mind and body reading. They were all more than twice my age and were at the top of their game in their area of expertise. I didn't stand a chance and George coerced me to stay at his house with Jim until the media backed off a bit. Luckily they weren't as aggressive as today's paparazzi. He assured me it was the right thing until I could decide on what to do. He said that I didn't want to drag this out in court and that Jim's attorney (Johnny Cochran) wasn't going to let Jim loose. They were trying to intimidate me and convince me that this could go away quietly if I listened to their advice. I wasn't trying to fight, I didn't know what was going on. They were doing damage control. This was the reason why women don't report these type of thing, especially when they are dealing with powerful men and later gave me understanding to why OJ didn't go to jail. As life would have it he payed later for something else. Jim could see I wasn't out for him. Yes, I was angry. I had just had the man that I loved beat me and now where do I put that love?! Jim started to cry and kept asking for me to forgive him and George told him to give me some time and for us to stay at his house for a few days and see where my mind was then. Funny thing, I believed that he was sorry but I wasn't going to let him off that easy. I needed to see, and I wasn't going to let it happen again. The good thing was Jim knew that I would defend myself, but who wants to live with the possibility of having to use a gun as a means to keep peace in a relationship, that's just crazy! I knew the love of a man... and had the love of my father. And I wasn't the desperate type of woman, but that didn't mean that abuse couldn't happen to me. There isn't a special type of woman. It could happen to any woman and that was what I didn't know. A few days later as they'd probably predicted Jim and I went home.

The house was quiet, no Kimberly or Denise. Denise had packed her things and moved in with some friends of hers, and Kimberly had been given back to her mother (named Kim) by the authorities at children and youth services. Doreen was still staying in the guest house and Gloria was still employed there, but they were no where in sight for the moment. After a few days Jim had me contact the detective and let him know that I wouldn't be pressing charges, even though the detective wasn't in agreement with it. Of course I wasn't sure as well. It was awkward at first and I had to face the music of my mother. She had filled up his answering machine with questions and I could hear the worry in her voice. I would make the dreaded call to her and Jim even spoke to her and assured her that I was fine and this wasn't as bad as the media had portrayed (which wasn't true)! Her little girl had experienced a great deal and everyone back home and around the world was talking. My mother could handle that, however, she had no way of knowing that I truly was ok and no one could convince me at that time to leave him. The reporters kept calling the house and Jim was so happy to have me back, he spoke with a reporter named "Diane K. Shah" who had just featured a story on us right before the fight took place. He told them that everything was ok and was spun out of control. He told them that I was sitting right there beside him and she asked to speak to me and when Jim put me on the phone Diane replied "That could have been any body"! Which was very true, however I knew that it was me who they were speaking to and she printed that in her next article. She wrote a lot things that she just speculated, like when she did our first interview Jim told me to give her the spelling of my name. He meant Debra as in D-E-B-R-A vs D-E-B-O-R-A-H. She was implying as if Jim didn't know me. I could have been born with another spelling on my birth certificate. That was the things Jim used to tell me all the time that some reporters would do in order to sensationalize a story. There was a lot of flavoring done to some reports, like Diane said she (Debra) is 22, however she looks 15. Looking up my graduating class or license from the DMV could have easily verified my age. It just sold more stories with sensationalism. I just know "Good Black don't Crack"!

We stayed in hiding for about a month. Jim would go out for grocery's but not to many would be brave enough to ask him any questions. I got back into our routine and we started to travel again, things seemed to have improved. It would be a year before it reared it's ugly head again and believe me it DID!

By the following summer people were talking about anything else but me and Jim. Every now and then I would catch a look from someone but they'd quickly turn their head so Jim wouldn't catch them staring. He didn't back off from anyone. In between we would go to all sorts of events from tennis tournaments to celebrity golf tournament, even one in Arizona. We stayed at big resorts and beautiful hotels across the country. I was comfortable because of my exposure from my family growing up. My high school had a number of Un popular sports that most high schools weren't effort, such as golf, archery, we even had a riffle team!

Something was off. Not with us but my body I couldn't eat and was loosing weight so Jim took me to the hospital, we found out that I was pregnant. He was so excited I think it was because of Kimberly being gone or he thought it would be a good way to keep me there in his life, I wasn't sure. I tried to be happy but I wasn't I was always waiting for the other shoe to drop. I knew that a baby would make me stay in his life and I knew that our life together wasn't the idea environment for an innocent baby. I was feeling trapped and definitely afraid of what was to come of all of this. How did my life become so complicated?! I knew deep down exactly what it was but wasn't honest with myself about my choices that I made. I had the choice to protect myself by using birth control or better yet since I was a Christian, to stay abstain from sex until marriage, or better yet waited for God to send me the mate that He had ordained for me. The list could go on and on. So together we would make probably the worst mistake of our lives...we terminated the life of our baby. I was put to sleep just so I wouldn't remember the process, however it didn't escape the fact that I knew that it happened. I grew even more depressed. All I did for the next few months was lay out by the pool. I didn't leave the house much anymore which made Jim very concerned to what was happening to me. The woman he fell in love with was fading away mentally and physically. He kept me costly guarded and what ever projects that Jim worked on he took me with him. He got a role in an up and coming movie titled "The Running Man" featuring Arnold Schwarzenegger. That was the first professional set I was on for a big budget movie. They gave Jim his own trailer where I would stay in when I didn't watch scenes where they were blowing things up. I met all of the cast the first day and to my surprise

Mr. T. was so sweet and so was Arnold. Everyone was so nice and seemed to like having me on the set. Even Jim was happy and glad to have some work. He had just started with a new agent and she was new to the business, her name was Nancy Rainford and so was her agency. She got Jim a lot of work. I was still a little weak and tired from the termination and would go to the trailer for rest most days. Arnold took notice of this and I heard him say to Jim in private outside of Jim's trailer that if I came on set another day appearing down, for Jim not to come back to work. Arnold knew something was very wrong with my demeanor. So the last few days of taping Jim let me stay at home

One day I got the urge to get up and go back to church. I knew that I had left my roots because of living with a man outside of the institution of marriage which gave me such guilt that it made it difficult to even ask God for forgiveness, which was just plan stupid on my behalf. God knew everything about me, I was His child and He knew that I would make every mistake that I had made...even my future sins. So I got dressed and went to Bishop E. Blake's church. When I returned home I was feeling a little better and was reminded that I served a forgiving God. But no sooner than I got in the door I could see that Jim was angry, but what would it be this time. He should have been happy to see that something made me a bit stronger, however, he said to me, "Why would you listen to that man when you could listen to me"?! I had an answer but I knew that it wouldn't be the one he would have liked to hear or excepted. Jim wasn't at that time a godly man he relied on himself for everything. He thought his way was the best and only way for our lives and that wasn't true. I don't care how high anyone climbs the ladder of success I feel you always need God and if we had Him in our lives we'd might not be in our situation...

After Jim fussed about me going to church I knew that it wouldn't be good if I kept going, or at least for a while. Maybe somehow I would be able to persuade him to go with me. Later Jim asked me to go with him over Barry Gordy's house. I wasn't sure what for. He didn't say, he just wanted me to go with him. I declined and he went any way. He was only gone for about two hours before he returned home and I was in bed…not asleep but I was tired. Tired of my life and couldn't figure out how to make it better without leaving him. I didn't want to I loved him still very much. His mood wasn't any better, he took off his clothes and got in bed. He asked me if I was awake and I said yes. He said while he was there that he ran into a friend of mine Marc DeBarge and he told Jim to tell me "hi" and that he and his brothers had missed me and haven't seen me in a while. Well, I sat up and was excited to hear from Jim about my friend and was glad to learn that Marc was ok and apparently working on his music other than that why would he be at Mr. Gordy's house? My sitting up somehow showed Jim that I was excited to hear about Marc and his brothers and I was. Before that Jim wasn't aware of me even knowing them. I knew a lot of people in the business during that time. Jim's entire mood got even more explosive than ever before…he asked me if I wanted to be with that _igga, and I asked him what was he talking about? How did we get to this?! What about in our conversation turn him into a screaming monster that looked as if he were going to kill me…I knew that I wasn't going to stick around for this. I walked calmly to the bed room door and Jim asked where was I going, I told him to the kitchen when in fact I was making a run for it out the front door and into the garage to get in my car to leave. When Jim heard the door to the garage, he ran outside and hit the garage door control which brought the door down onto the roof of my jeep. The bars stopped the door from crushing my jeep, however it ripped the cloth top. Then he ran around to the drivers side and shoved me over and tried to pull the jeep back inside the garage all while we were fighting over the gear shift. I knew if he got me back inside the house it was not going to end well for me. While he was trying to get the gear in shift I jumped out of the passenger side and made a run for it up the driveway. Jim left the jeep running

and ran up the driveway right behind me. Because he was much
faster than I was he caught up to me right before I was at the top
and grabbed hold of my legs and I came down face first on the
curb between the paving and the yard! We both were in shock. I
was bleeding from my total face. I couldn't say from exactly where,
I could not see myself or even feel pain. He immediately picked
me up and brought me into the house where I was fighting to get
him to let go of me. My blood was smeared all over the doorway
and walls. I grabbed hold of everything I could in order to not
get trapped back into his house, but his strength over powered
me. This time he didn't have a look of anger, it was FEAR!!! He
knew he had done something awful! My teeth were gone. I was so
swollen that I looked like a monster. I was Un recognizable! Jim had
panache. He reached into his drawer and took out his gun. He was
saying…"No body would believe this was an accident and now I
have to kill us both"! But it wasn't an accident. If he hadn't beaten
me before and always getting angry about something or another,
I wouldn't have been afraid enough to run! He kept putting the
gun in my mouth and then putting it to his head. He went back
and forth with this for several times. He was out of his mind and
panache! Somehow I knew that I was going to survive and get out
of this…dying was not an option for me. What should have been a
horrible time I somehow had a peace and that came from God. If I
didn't have peace and control over myself and panache along with
Jim there was a great possibility that he would have killed us both!
Then he got on the phone and made a call, that was when I went
in the bathroom to take a look. OH MY GOD…what did he do to
me I thought! I couldn't see myself anywhere. I was swollen from
my forehead to my chin and the blood was all over my face and my
two front teeth were missing. I could see why he was so panache
for the first time. He kept me at gun point in the bed room until it
got dark, that was when the pain kicked in and it was horrible! He
gave me two pills to take for the pain and the next thing I knew is
that I woke up the next day with the same "Night Mare"! Jim was
still sitting on the bed holding the gun, trying to figure out what

to do. He put some of our clothes in an overnight bag grabbed a bag of money and when he did, I went outside and walked to the place where it happened and behold there was my teeth! Both of them completely in tact from the root! They had still had some of my flesh and blood with ants crawling all over them. I picked them up and placed them in some tissue paper and put them in my back pocket of my jeans. I didn't try to escape even though Jim was in the house. Where was I to go in that condition?! I felt like I now needed him, he had the money to get this fixed. I didn't know who could make me right again! The press would have me all over the place looking like a monster for everyone to see. What could I do...everyone told me to leave him! I was ashamed even though I didn't do myself the physical harm, but ignoring the warnings from everyone left me in this predicament. All I could think of was surviving and getting repaired! I went back into the house and into our bathroom and washed off my teeth and placed them into a clean tissue and back into my back pocket. Jim and I got into his car and drove off. I didn't know where we were going and didn't care or asked. He drove us up the coast to Santa Barbara.

I stayed in the car while he got us checked into a hotel. I didn't want anyone to see me looking like this. By this time I even had black eyes along with my swelling. I can't explain why I didn't scream for help. Somehow I thought because of his celebrity no one would. Or worst yet I would have been mocked for being a fool for staying. I felt helpless with no where to go!

We stayed in the hotel for two more days. I saw that he still had the gun, however he must have known that I wasn't going to flee. My swelling has subsided some, enough to go out in public without most noticing that I was beaten, only if I kept my mouth closed so no one would see that my teeth were missing. We mostly ordered in except for the one time we walked on the beach and the gardens at the hotel. They were beautiful. Funny how I could still see the beauty of the things God created while I was suffering in such physical pain, except when Jim gave me the pain medication at night so I could rest. Before we left the hotel I convinced Jim to take me to a dentist.

Jim made arrangements with a Dr. Michael Luther in Culver City. We headed to his office in the middle of the night. When we arrived at Dr. Luther's office it was quiet because there was no one there beside the three of us. He was a short dark complexioned black man. He said as little as possible, probable afraid of what he had gotten himself into.
He told me that I was very lucky that they came out in one piece and that my nerves were still alive, I knew that that was God's grace. He put my teeth back in and reinforced them with braces until they set. He never gave me a time line on just how long that would take and he never asked me what occurred to me to make that happen…he knew! I didn't care what he asked me or not, all I could think of is that I had my teeth! He gave me instructions on how to care for my teeth some pain medication and anti biotic to keep out any infections. By the time we left his office it would be day light. But before we left I saw Jim hand Dr. Luther a brown bag of money. I wonder how much Jim paid for Dr. Luther's silence…

We were on our way back home when I asked Jim to pull over at a taco stand to see if I could get some straws at the counter. I never thought about purchasing some at a grocery store. He pulled over and I asked one of the employee's if it were alright to take some and he replied yes, when I did a LAPD officer was there apparently getting something to eat himself asked me if I was having a party? I replied no and stated that I just had dental surgery. Jim was sitting in the car and over heard the officer's statement to me and got out of the car to make him apologize to me. I was confused, I didn't know why Jim was angry and felt a need to correct him. When we got in the car Jim explained that the officer implied that I was getting the straws for a party that would be using cocaine! He and the officer both missed the mark. If the officer paid closer attention to me just having surgery on my mouth and getting in the car with a man known for abuse he might have put two and two together! Even if he did I still might have not left. My scars weren't just physical they were now emotional. How did I let that happen?!

When we got to the house I notice that my blood was all cleaned up by our house keeper Gloria. She was glad to see me and I know it was because of her returning to work after her weekend off to find us not there and blood all over the place wondering what happened and was I still alive. She later told me that she thought I was dead and Mr. Brown was on the run or something. I didn't expect for her to tell the press or anything Gloria was very loyal to me for hiring her, but Jim paid her and she knew that this was an opportunity for her to pay her bills and bring her daughter over to the United States. Gloria was from Guatemala. Her loyalty to Jim over the years he helped her and her daughter become legal citizens and for her daughter to go to college. As for as I know Gloria is still employed by Jim.

Jim monitored my use of the pain medication so I wouldn't get hooked on it. I never liked any use of legal or street drugs. I was healing good. I used a trick that my mother had given us in my youth to hold Listerine and peroxide in my mouth every time that I got a chance to and also to hold warm salt water as well. My gums were attaching back to my teeth, I could feel it.

A few weeks later I got a call out of the blue from my grandma Daisy, She was my biological father's mother. She told me that the doctor's gave my father only a few weeks to live and that he was dying of cancer. She wanted to see if I could fly to New York to see him before that took place. So I asked Jim if that was possible because I knew that Jim was having financial trouble. Because of his guilt he said yes, but he was very reluctant because he didn't want anyone to see what had happened to me. Everyone knew that I didn't have braces before this. I told him that my excuse would be is that I wanted to close up the gap I had in my teeth, so Jim booked my flight.

New York looked the same, but not as dirty as it was in the early 1970's. I took a taxi to Harlem and my father was waiting and very happy to see me. I was at least 3 or 4 years since he had. And since last year when I made the news with Jim with him beating me I hadn't seen anyone in my family, but my father told me he didn't have a need because I did what he expected of me...I defended myself and he could hardly get the laugh out but I could see his body jerking in a laughing motion when he tried to get out about me shooting at Jim. He said that I know that _otha _ucker ran like he was on a football field dodging those bullets! Just like he taught me to never let a man put their hands on me. But why was I still there and how come I haven't seemed to recover from it, and my father knew that I was still being abused and then he(my father) asked me something that I hadn't expected at all...Do you want him dead?! This was a gift from my father that I didn't need to cash in! It was validation for all of the recitals he'd missed and child support he didn't pay. It was him covering me as a father against the battle he knew that I couldn't win without him intervening or Gods! My father knew that he had only a few weeks to live and was going to make up for anything that he missed in my life and was going to make it right before he left this earth and if that meant killing Jim Brown then that was what he was going to do! We stopped walking in the middle of the side walk and I turned to him and said daddy I want you to get into the Kingdom of Heaven and I know if you commit murder that is a sin against God, and he replied I will kill that _igga and deal with Jesus when I see Him! I never questioned the love from my father again and Jim is alive because of me telling my father not to kill him. To this day Jim doesn't know God graced his life by me saying no. That was the strength I took back with me to Los Angeles when I returned! I never needed another mans love for me, I had my fathers. And my Heavenly Fathers as well but yet to discover that! When I flew back I had a power that was rising up on the inside of me. The me that I once knew was coming back. Knowing that I had the power to make Jim pay was enough, but if I hold my peace and let the Lord fight my battle it would turn out the way God would attend for it to be...and God would not only repay Jim but would restore and empower me to leave, but not before some more lessons.

I wasn't back home one week before my father would pass away which made me so glad that I took the time to go and see about him. That visit with him was a pivotal point in my life and the strength to keep fighting for my life. I asked Jim to book me another flight and he said no, and that I got to see my father before he passed and that he kept it private that he didn't have the money. I didn't care and I told him that I was going and I didn't care how he came up with the money that he wasn't going to make me miss my fathers funeral! Nothing was going to keep me from it! So off I went back to New York.

My father's family were from the streets and empowered me some more by laughing at the stories that they read in the papers that I shot at Jim when he put his hands on me. My Aunt Betty Anne said that Jim probably didn't know that his running back skills would come in handy with helping him dodge all those bullets! She laughed so hard you'd thought she was at a comedy club! My sister Lisa would be the only one to question my braces, I gave her the story I told Jim and I knew that she wasn't going for it! Lisa was always inquisitive, she knew when things weren't right. It was good seeing all of my family and we all got along for once. I was missing them on my return to LA.

About a month had past and my sister Lisa called Jim and invited herself out. She was noisy and wanted to see what was going on there for herself! She even made Jim pay for her flight... Lisa had/has moxie! That was the thing about my family we could fight each other but no one else better touch one of us without us sticking up for one another, and that is how we still roll. When she arrived Jim picked her up from the airport by himself, I stayed back at the house. Like Lisa always in rare form she came in the door fussing and arguing with Jim. She was standing up for me and wasn't backing down from what she thought was going on. She didn't care that he was bigger or stronger than herself, she was going to protect her baby sister at any and all cost. I couldn't understand then and wanted for her to stop. I wanted for her to see the beauty of LA and our home and all that LA had to offer. She wasn't having it and it took her a while to settle down. Funny thing Jim did every thing in his power to make her have a great time. He took us every where and even gave his check book to Lisa and I to let us go shopping and get what ever we desired and Lisa declined. She was proud and told him that he couldn't buy her respect or love, that he should have just treated me right! She told him that her sister could have had anybody and did, and that he was lucky to have me! She saw right through Jim's insecurities and read him thoroughly! Now it was he who was afraid. Afraid of what I was getting from my sister...my power back. The last day of Lisa's visit Jim took us to the "Play Boy Mansion". That was a fun time with Lisa. She had never followed the rules and did the same there. Mr. Hefner had a pond full of Japanese fish that swam on the back of their tails when fed. You only needed just a pinch of feed to see them do this. I told Lisa and she took two fist full of the feed and threw it as high as she could into the air and the fish jumped out so high into the air to catch the feed, some even were on the grass flopping around our feet. It scared us half to death we went running and screaming away from the fish. I took her all around the grounds and showed her all of the wild animals that were kept at the "Playboy Mansion". Lisa taunted the monkeys and chased the peacocks that roamed the grounds freely and we laughed and ran when some of them wasn't having it and chased us back. That was the first time I witnessed Lisa enjoying her trip. I couldn't tell if Mr. Hefner liked Lisa because he was always a gracious host, however I know that he was entertained by her. Like everyone that had come before Lisa, her stay came to an end. I know that Jim was glad and hoped that I didn't have anymore sisters to come and visit.

The holidays were coming around and Jim had made secret plans for them. I wanted a tree and couldn't understand why he kept telling me no. I insisted and then decorated the entire living room including the fire place. Jim was glad anyhow because it made the house festive when his guest came by like his friend Booker and wife. He told me later that he was glad that I decorated. We had a lot of visitors during the holidays. Jim's two sons Jim, James and his other daughter Kimberly children from Jim's first wife who was now living in Atlanta Georgia. She was married to him when he was playing for the "Cleveland Brown's". They had a look of confusion because they were all older than me. The only child that Jim had that was younger than me was his youngest daughter Kimberly. To clear up the confusion to why he had two daughters named Kimberly the first was by his first wife and the second by his ex-girlfriend named Kim who named their daughter after herself. Jim told them that they were welcome to visit more ofter, all in all it was a good visit. However, Kimberly would be the only one of them that I saw again after that. Christmas was just around the corner and Jim and I were laying in bed and pulled out a box and told me to open it. I didn't want to because I told him that I wanted something to open up Christmas morning. He told me to open it anyway. I was so excited I couldn't guess to what it might be and when did he go shopping and I thought he was still having financial troubles, so I dare not expect anything. I was happy with his love and that was enough for me. I wished that he knew that. When things were good they were good. Jim made me laugh and our love to me was wonderful, if only he could control his abusive ways. We enjoyed so many of the same things. We were both natural athletes and very competitive. We challenged each other in everything from cooking to roller blading. He even challenged me the first time I got well to jump off his roof into the pool and I did! He thought when I got up there I would see just how high it was and back off. I never turned down a challenge which I think to this day which was what made me stay so long. I thought he would know that I loved him and that would make him stop. I opened the box and it was a beautiful diamond bangle tennis bracelet. It was 14k yellow gold. Jim put it on my wrist and that's when he had a look of surprise that I was so small. He made a comment that maybe he should have given me something else instead so it wouldn't fall off of my wrist.

I told him no and that it was perfect and that I loved it, however I hoped that I wouldn't loose it. He told me what he had another surprise for us and for me to hurray up and get packed that we were leaving for Hawaii in the morning. I gave him a big kiss and jumped out of the bed to pack. After I got packed and got back into the bed we made love and afterwards I kept staring at my new gift while he spooned me. I though everything was going to work out in that moment...all was good, I was so excited that I don't recall falling asleep.

We flew to "Wi Kiki" and like a child I could hardly wait until we got checked into the hotel so we could go to the beach. Jim could see that this was not money waisted for sure. I was like a child on Christmas morning. Before this I had never been to any island. The sun and sand was my thing. After we did our usual stop in the room we hurried and changed for the beach. The sand was as soft as anything I could have ever expected and so white. It was blinding from the sun and the reflection of the sun off of the ocean. We laid out on our blanket in the sand. And I said to Jim that I was glad that he planned this surprise for me and it was the best Christmas I'd ever had, but he knew that the surprises wasn't yet over, he had more up his sleeve. One of the couples we knew had come as well, Julian and her boyfriend Mario(who owned a club called "Vertigo" in the Beverly Centre) They met us out on the beach. We had a blast all day in the sun except for a thought I had when I saw a baby running around naked playing in the sand. His bottom was pink from sun burn and Jim caught me steering at the toddle playing and whispered to me...we will have one too. He knew that I was having regrets of our abortion and wasn't going to let it stop me from enjoying our vacation. I was sad when he said it because of my other thought...that it might not be with him. I didn't know if I was going to stay...I didn't know if he would change. I was loosing hope that he would.

Later that evening we had diner and I was tired from all of the travel and sun I wanted to go back to the room and sleep, but Jim wanted to go where the music was playing in the hotel. They had a night club. So reluctantly I went with him. We were seated in a VIP section and watched the people dancing. I noticed a lot of the people were Japanese. Actually the hotel was owned by them and a great deal of the island. I asked Jim how could that be and where were all of the locals. I just figured out that I hadn't seen much locals that entire day. Jim explained to me that anyone could buy property anywhere if you had the money. I just assumed that the Hawaiians would own everything since it was their land. He was always teaching me and said that we would go to local spots and share their experience. The next day we would walk around the beach and shopping areas. At that time I wasn't a huge shopper, Jim filled all of my desires, but it was making someone jealous other than Jim and that was God. He said for us not to put any other gods before Him and that was what I was doing. We were both doing it. We were each others everything and that wasn't good. Every now and then Jim was spotted by fans, but he always knew how to handle it. He explained to them that we too were on vacation and said if he'd start signing autographs that we would spend most of our vacations with him working. Most of them understood that concept. We did however, stop for a photographer who had his own small business and asked us to pose with his parrots. I told Jim that the photographers assistant kept telling the parrot to pinch my shoulder with it's claws and Jim didn't believe me until he saw my shoulder after we took the picture. I knew she told the bird to that some woman didn't like seeing Jim with such a younger woman. They thought that I was a gold digger.I had another experience like that with "Ester Roll" she was the mother on the tv show "Good Times". We were at a fund raiser "Danny Glover" had to bring awareness to "Apartheid". For what was to come next will show you, you can't make or buy love.

Jim and I would take a small chartered jet to another island "Kwai" the next day. He was invited by the owner of the new golf coarse that they were building. When we arrived, we were met by the owner and he took us to the spec house which looked like a log cabin made of mostly wood. It sat in the middle of some greenery with nothing but the golf corse around it. They didn't seem to care that it was rainy, all the owner seemed to care about is that Jim was there and he could impress his friends. I am certain that Jim was aware of that and he was used to the politics of being a celebrity, actually he was a master at it. No one controlled him, he was definitely his own man. He probable knew that he could make some connections and play some golf for free. I didn't want to escort him on the field because of the rain so I stayed back with the wives of the men. I was swarmed with questions and most probably didn't understand the dynamics of our relationship, I could tell by the questions, however, they were very gracious. After which seemed about all day the men returned and Jim stayed long enough to eat and we took the jet back to "Wi Kiki". The flight was very crowded. There were others traveling back with us. The plane was carrying about a dozen people all together including us. It was a very rough flight with a lot of turbulence. I was extremely nervous. I thought what a terrible time for my life to end just when things were getting good between Jim and I. He must have known what I was thinking and right at the point of me screaming to get us down and out of that airplane, Jim pulled out a diamond ring and proposed to me in the middle of all of that turbulence. What a way to distract me from that frightening moment, heck it distracted everyone on the plane. Everyone was within ear shot of him doing this. I was so surprised and gladly excepted and he put the most beautiful ring on my finger! The condition was for us to get married while we were there. Everyone applauded and were congratulating us both and before we knew it our tiny aircraft had landed. When our plane landed on the tarp everyone waited for us to get out to take pictures. Now what would be my excuse to leave...things were good. It all seemed like a wonderful dream and, still does to this very day. If it weren't for the jewelry, photos, news articles, and other nice things I would have though it was all a dream. The highs were so high and the lows were some of the lowest points in my life. I still haven't found out just how can a person who you love so much hurt you the most. Why didn't he figure out how not to chase me out of his life. He would often cry and ask me never to leave him but knew that I would eventually. But for now I agreed to get married the following day. We went back to the hotel had diner and went to bed. We made love and that goes without saying. I don't know of a day that we didn't except for the days when I had my menstrual cycle and the two surgeries. We were crazy about each other and saw that as a way of being close. The next morning Jim did what he said we were to go visit the local side of the island. We stopped at some market places and rode side shops. I even purchased some Maui onions to take back home. They were so good you can eat them like an apple, some locals did. We came upon a beach were the local men were body surfing and I didn't see any other people in the ocean. Jim and I walked down to the beach and I stood in the shallow and the water was very ruff. It was almost cutting me. It was something called a riptide that was causing the sand under the water to cut my skin, so I got out. I sat on the beach in my clothes and watched Jim as the local men were giving him instructions on how to body surf. Jim was confident that he could do it since he was an athlete and was the weight of most of the local men and Jim was in great shape for a man of 49-50. He caught on fast and was body surfing like the rest of the men, however, they all must have gotten quite comfortable because of Jim athleticism, that they never payed attention to when Jim never came up out of the ocean. I stood up when I could no longer see him. Then others noticed as well. I ran closer to the ocean and was panache. I couldn't see where he was. The local men too took notice and began diving under the water searching for him...oh God...where was he! It felt like Jim was must have been under the water for about 2-3 minuets and washed up about two-fifths of a mile down the beach. He was face down and very still. There was no movement coming from his body. All of the local man and a few other people who were on the beach where his body washed up surrounded him and was assessing him. I quickly ran over. I had to break through the crowd of people and that was always a problem for me, Jim always handled the crowd and this time he couldn't he wasn't moving. No one would move out of my way so Jim could know that I was there. When I finally made it threw, I could see that his face was scrapped up from him getting dragged along the bottom of the ocean from the riptide. The scrape on his forehead was in the shape of a cross. It went across his forehead and straight down the middle of his nose. There was some sort of a medic and they were handling his immediate care along with the much experienced local surfer men. They knew exactly what happened to Jim and what to do. What took place all happened in about 20 minuets from the time Jim got in the ocean until he washed up on shore, it felt like an eternity. I was so glad when Jim could sit up and the first thing he asked me is..."Where were you, I kept thinking to myself..."where is Debra". I thought that I would be the last thing he thought of before he might of died and the first thing he thought of when he didn't! That was how much we loved each other! Jim was a very proud man and refused any treatment from the medics. He just wanted to get back to our hotel room. He tried to lean on me, however I was much too small to support his weight...which let me know that he was truly injured! We whisked passed the managers in the lobby and went straight to our room. Word had travelled that fast back to the hotel. I could tell that Jim didn't want that kind of attention. We stayed in our room for the duration of our trip.

I watched Jim from our room, he spent last bit of time in Hawaii out on the balcony watching the ocean and the sun set. They were beautiful! We both didn't say much, he seemed to be in deep thought. He took some pain medication and we went to bed. The next day we departed Hawaii, I couldn't even think about the engagement or anything good that happened. I could tell that Jim had a lot of discomfort on the plain ride back to Los Angeles. He should have upgraded our flight so he could get more comfortable. I think that he just wanted to get home. He shared something with me on the way home that he now knew what I must have felt like when he attacked me…He told me that he felt helpless against the ocean and how big the ocean was compared to him, and how big in comparison he is to me. And that the scar left on his forehead would remind him to never put his hands on me again. I don't recall him actually saying the word sorry, however that was enough for me to know he felt convicted of it. After we landed we got a limo home.

When we arrived at the gate Jim had to get out to unlock it to let the limo driver into the property. We got our things and went straight to our room. I laid down on the bed I was tired from all the travel. Jim put the luggage in our room and walked straight back to the living room. I heard voices coming from the area. I knew no one was there. We gave Gloria the time off for the holiday and Denise had moved out and Doreen when to stay with family or something of the sort. The next thing I knew Jim had this girl that I had only seen one other time at the house on an occasion of some sort. She was swimming in our pool completely naked. She was laughing and seemed very disturbed. Not caring that she somehow let herself in our property without any permission. Jim wasn't in any sort of mood to be bothered with this type of nonsense. He grabbed her and her things up to the top of the driveway and locked her out. These type of occurrences were common place in "Hollywood". He didn't even bother to call the police. He got in bed with me and we went to sleep.

That night I had the strangest dream. It was Jim my sister Lisa and myself. We were all out on the balcony of Jim's house and were looking out over the city, when the sky started to turn weird colors of pink and orange then the sky started to wrestle with itself. It was twisting and the clouds which were the same colors looked as if they were tying into a knot...then the sky split open and there He was...

It was Jesus's face as big as the sky above. There is a scripture that says: "The earth is His footstool and the fullness thereof". Maybe that is why He appeared to me so large?! I knew one thing I wasn't living a life that was pleasing to God and I wasn't ready for Christ return! I sat up immediately out of my sleep! My heart was racing and I was short of breath. I was so unnerved that I startled Jim. He asked me if I were ok and when I looked at him I could see small horns on his head. Not the pointed kind, the kind that was shaped sort of like two small pyramids, but not as pointed. I wasn't sure if I was still sleeping because of what I saw. I had never seen any type of vision before in my life! I told Jim that I was all right and he asked me if I had a bad dream and I said yes but wouldn't look at him. I pulled the covers over my head and tried to figure out if I was still dreaming. A few minuets past by and I needed to use the bathroom, so I got up and looked at him again and the horns were still there. I used the bathroom and came back to bed and the horns never left Jim's head. I was now afraid of him and what in the world was going on with me? Was it a premonition of some sort or was I still dreaming or was it a warning from God for me to get out! I thought the latter of the three. I told Jim that I needed to leave. I don't know what he thought and didn't care. He asked me what was wrong and tried to come to some sort of compromise. He said that we could move to Georgia and that California wasn't good for us and he would call his mother (Theresa) in St. Simons Island, Georgia to make arrangements for me to go ahead to see if I liked it. I had spoken to Jim's mother on the phone a few times before this and Jim agreed to make the arrangements. He didn't know what was wrong with me but didn't want me to be out of his life. Neither did I, however, I knew if I stayed that I might not live and/or live the kind of life God had intended for me. I got on the flight to Theresa's home in St. Simons Island, Georgia. Funny thing when I arrived even though she and I never met before this, we knew each other right away. She told me that I fit the type of her sons mold and she looked to me just like Jim but with a wig. She was a big strapping woman. We got in her car and drove which seemed to be a very long time. When we got closer to her home she rode me past local places and shops. She did most of the talking and asked me if I needed anything before we got to the house. She seemed to be glad that I was there but wasn't sure what her role was going to be with me. Does she keep me pre-occupied until Jim comes, or does she just try to heal and comfort me as a mother. However she was what I needed at the time...a safe place to lay my head.

She took me into a tiny wood framed white house that was in need of a paint job. It sat on stilts above ground level, but was a one story house. It was built for that reason for flooding since they were near water. St. Simons Island is a beautiful place. Untouched by man. Theresa carried my bag in and showed me where I would be sleeping. I asked her if she mind if I had laid down and she said "no baby get some rest"! I laid down on one of those old fashioned brass framed bed with the best down feather mattresses and pillows from back in the day, with the most crisp white cotton sheets and a home made patchwork quilt. I slept like I hadn't in years!

When I woke up I could hear Theresa on the phone. I could tell that she was talking to Jim. She kept telling him that I wasn't well and life with him or what ever it was wasn't good and that she was concerned for me. She wasn't trying to upset Jim. She knew that I was the reason why they had gotten back into communicating. I had found some letters before in the basement when I purchased a new washer and dryer and hot water tank from "Big Bear". I found a stack of letters addressed to Jim unopened and from a Theresa Brown. I thought she was an ex-wife and confronted Jim with the letters and he explained it was his mother. I made him call her to prove it and that was how they started talking again. She did not want to jeopardize that and I didn't want that to happen either. She tried to explain to him that what ever was going on out there wasn't good for me. When she realized that I was awake she got off the phone. She came into the bed room and asked me if I was hungry and that she had fried some fish for me. I didn't have much of an appetite but the fish smelled so good that it was probably the reason I woke up. She was a good cook. We sat there at the kitchen table and she opened up to me. She told me that she knew her son very well and how he treated woman and that she was risking her relationship with him by talking to me about this matter. God knew that Theresa would be the only person that could reach me. She had every thing to loose (her relationship with her son and her extra income that Jim provided for her). And because her only relationship to him was to be his mother, I knew she wasn't trying to manipulate me in order to get something from me like most people who were in our circle. She wouldn't have gained anything by helping me escape his grip. So I entrusted her with the decision and plan. She then asked me if I had family and where they lived and if she could call someone on my behalf. The next thing I knew, Theresa had called my mother and shared her thoughts about Jim and my relationship. My mother agreed that she didn't think it was good however, she didn't insist on me coming home and said that I was of age to make my own decisions. I sometimes thought it was about money. Jim gave me money every two weeks to send via "Western Union" to both of our mothers. He did that for quite some time and if I returned home that might have all stopped. But my eldest sister Lisa took the phone from my mother and insisted that I should come home. Lisa made arrangements with Jim's mother Theresa and wrote a bounce check to the airlines and met me in Atlanta. We stayed with one of my moms friends daughter's house.I never traveled with money, except the times I travelled to New York to see about my father and then my fathers funeral. Jim was always with me and I never wanted for a thing that he wasn't willing to provide. Jim was a good provider. He even purchased me a car before we were dating. He wanted to make sure that I got to work safely. My sister and I were trying to figure out how would we get back to Pittsburgh. I told my sister that I always kept a check book of Jim's, but I was only to use it for expenses for the house or something I needed, and she said…"You are in need and you need to get home before he kills you"! So she talked me into writing a check and I cashed it at a bank in Atlanta to purchase us tickets back home to Pittsburgh. I was at my mothers house in just a day.

I didn't feel the warm welcome that one would think I should have gotten from my family. No one knew what to do with me. I called Theresa to let her know that I made it back and she told me that Jim was angry with her and blamed her for helping me leave. I told her that I was sorry that their relationship had been damaged once more and she told me not to worry about that and for me to get better. I told her that I would stay and touch and she told me that I probably wouldn't, however that she understood. That I would probably want to for get the entire thing. But before we hung up she told me that he was looking for me and probably was on his way to Pittsburgh. I figured as much.

He did call. I heard Jim on the phone with my mother. She wasn't nice to him and told him how unhealthy I looked. I was naturally thin and by this time I was looking anorexic. I was so weak. I had no zeal for life anymore. I was being controlled by him and didn't have to be. I loved him but couldn't live like that anymore, but what could I do? I felt I would die without him but couldn't live with him. It seemed that we could have made it together if we got some sort of council. Minister Farrakhan was one of Jim's closest friends. That was a problem for why we couldn't be counseled by him, Jim was his peer and wouldn't have allowed a man who he knew personally to tell him what to do. We spent a lot of time with the Minister at our home and even stayed with the Minister in Arizona. I knew his wife and two of his sons. I recall two frightening times we spent with the Minister.

One when we visited with him in Arizona and he spoke at some auditorium and we kept getting bomb threats and kept having to clear the auditorium. Another time the Minister came over and Jim had just roughed me up and the Minister clearly saw that I looked disheveled and he didn't say a word to Jim, which let me know that the Minister's relationship with Jim was man to man. I don't think Jim had a friend who might have challenged him in that area except for Richard Pryor. The only bad thing is that Jim's response would be to tell Richard that he had his own set of problems, and that would shut the whole thing down. So here I was back in my childhood bed room. This didn't feel good either, knowing that I had been all around the world and landed back in my childhood bed room somehow just didn't seem right. Jim would take the next flight out to Pittsburgh. When he arrive at my mothers house I wanted to jump in his arms but my feet wouldn't move. He could see that I was broken. He sat at the kitchen table with my mother and she made him look at all the pictures of my childhood and that I had a promising future and if he truly loved me he needed to let me go. He sat there and cried in front of my mother and I. I felt sorry for him and didn't want my mother to humiliate him in front of me. He took it all in for the first time. I felt bad because I watched him do so much for the people around me, some who were my friends and others I didn't know myself. He did those things to make me happy. Everyone seemed to take advantage of him loving me. They enjoyed the food, parties, pool and where he would take them. It was all a big mess.

My mother suggested for me to take Jim to my high school and show him all that I had accomplished as a youth and that I had a promising future. I was recognized at my school and accomplished a great deal in sports, cheerleading, dance and pageants. He and I took my mothers car and drove up to my school. We sat there in the car looking at the school grounds so he my get some idea of who I was before him. When we returned to the house my mother had made diner, we ate and then Jim and

I climbed into one of the twin beds in my room. I was so small that we both fit comfortably. He spooned me and I felt safe and at home with him again. I felt safe because he would never blow up on me in my mothers house. I felt safe like the times before he hit me, where his touch was about love and it comfort me. Were would we go from here. We seemed doomed. I didn't know long term where I was going but I knew short term I was going to church in the morning to find some answers. I got ready for church in the morning and my sister Lisa picked me up. We both sang in the choir and she was still was in our choir so we left out early. I sat in the choir and was welcomed since I knew most of the songs and I knew there was healing singing to the Lord. The next thing that I knew, in walks Jim. He wore his white suit and white Nike tennis shoes. I knew that he wore tennis shoes a lot because of they were more comfortable since he was a little beat up from playing sports. Pastor Lauren E. Mann gave Jim a nod of acknowledgement when Jim walked in and kept at his sermon. I didn't know if he would even come. I never asked him. It always seemed to be a problem if I went to church when I lived with Jim back in California, so I never thought to ask him. Even though Pastor Mann didn't make a big deal out of Jim walking in, it was difficult for Jim to walk in any where without people noticing. He was big in stature and very noticeable being he is a star and notable athlete. I could see all of the congregation talking and whispering that Jim was there and I was trying not to focus on the gossip of the congregation. It made me angry to see them perched up about his celebrity. They seemed to have forgotten he abused me. Celebrity effects most people in a weird way. Their judgement seems to go right out of the window. I've seen people do some crazy things around celebrities that they might not have done. When church was over and before I could go over to Jim he was surrounded by the people in my church. Some wanted autographs, others just wanted to see him up close. My Pastor came over to him and shook his hand and thanked Jim for coming to worship with us and that he was always welcomed anytime he was in town. Jim came to church because he had an agenda. He asked Pastor Mann to marry us right now. I was shocked. I watched Pastor Mann step in as a father figure, in fact he told Jim that he was making a decision for me as a father since he knew that my father had passed on to be with the Lord. Pastor Mann told Jim that he wouldn't marry us not now or ever. I couldn't believe neither man considered what I wanted. I felt that my life was being negotiated by everyone except me. Even though I knew that I didn't have the ability at that time to make a sound decision for myself. I couldn't believe Pastor Mann told Jim that to his face. He might not have been aware that Jim might not have taken that well and didn't have a respect for clergy men and saw him just as a man and might have shown him physically. I guess that Jim and I both knew that we had made so many mistakes and that might not have made things any better by getting married that day. We went back to my mothers house and Jim told me that he needed to get back to LA and asked me to come back home with him. God knows I wanted to, but what grantee would I have that I would be safe, there wasn't one. That was a difficult thing not to get on the plane with Jim. He returned home by himself.

Later that week I got a call from someone at "Continental Airlines". They said that they tried to reach me while I was in LA. They were recruiting Flight Attendant " positions and had a training class starting soon in Newark, New Jersey and would I like to come on board. I believe to this very day that was a gift from God. I could control my emotions at the time and this was an escape to keep me occupied until my heart healed. They sent me a ticket to fly to New Jersey and I started a 6 week training program that took all of my attention and motivation. In fact I liked it. I did talk to Jim and I could tell that he wasn't truly happy for me, he just wanted me to come home. I did want to go back however, I needed to complete the training and see if I could get Jim out of my system. When I completed all of my training my first trip was to London, England. It was an 8 day trip. That was the largest aircraft that I had been on and I would spend a good amount of time in Europe. Our phone calls became routine. Every time I would call him he asked for me to come home. Having a job was a way for me to be in control. I could fly in whenever I missed him and I could leave whenever I felt threatened. One particular time I had a 14 day rip from Newark with stop overs in Los Angeles, Hawaii then Australia and back again. Everyone desired to get this assigned trip. So I decided to surprise Jim on my over night in LA. I caught a cab from my hotel near the airport to his house and when I got there Mike Tyson answered the door. He had a huge smile on his face and said for me to come in. I asked where Jim was and he said that he would be right back. I could see there was another man in the living room from where I was standing in the doorway. It was "Big Daddy Kane" he was a rapper who beat women as well. I knew that because I had met his girlfriend Dawn while I was living in New Jersey. As a matter of fact they all were, "Birds of a feather flock together"! I turned around and ran for the cab that was still turning around in the driveway. I wasn't going to find out what might have happened to me should I stayed and waited for Jim. I was getting wiser. When I got back to the hotel, Jim had called me and asked for me to come back. I told him that I would in a few days after I came back from Hawaii and Australia. After about 5 days I would stop pass Jim's on the way back. He made sure that there wouldn't be anyone there but he and Gloria. She was glad to see me and would tell me how much Jim had missed me and how he was so sad he was without me. I missed him too, I missed our entire life together I would have traded anything to bring it back without the dangers of being abused. There wasn't any guarantee, I had to keep moving. Jim was like a drug the more I kept going back it made it harder each time that I left. I was so tired of the traveling and I went to visit my doctor to see why I was so tired all the time. I was pregnant and when I shared it with my job, they told me the dangers of flying in the first and last trimester. The cabin pressure can cause a miscarriage if you have had previous problems with pregnancy. But if I left my job how would I support myself and my baby? I wasn't sure if it was Jim's baby. I had dated a guy in New Jersey just to see if I could somehow fall out of love with Jim. I seemed to keep making mistakes that were attached to him somehow. I made most of my decisions based around "if this could keep me from going back to Jim". I kept my pregnancy hidden from him and got a job in my church. I worked in the daycare, what a way of God preparing me for mother hood. However, it wouldn't be enough money to sustain my life with a baby. My girlfriend BethAnne and sister Lisa came to visit me and along with my church they gave me a beautiful baby shower. Not long after Bianca was born, I found out that she had a lot of health problems. She suffered a stroke and seizures by not getting enough oxygen to her brain during delivery. I asked Jim for financial help so I could get better medical treatment for her. He told me that the only way that he would help is if I came back. I couldn't imagine taking my new innocent baby into such a situation. What if Jim used her as a tool to control me?! Bianca needed serious medical treatment and was advised for us to see a neurologist at children's hospital in Pittsburgh, PA. This was fate, I was taking my baby home, not to LA, but to Pittsburgh. Dr. Jarjour was wonderful and got her great treatment and I got enrolled in every service they had to insure her recovery. Later I learned that she had more complications, and put all of my energy into getting her healthy. She was the cutest baby and never gave me a moments problem. I found something that I loved more than Jim, my baby. He would still come to visit me, and I believe he wanted to see Bianca for himself to see if there was a resemblance. He wanted to see if she was his and that would be the way of getting me home.

I enrolled back in school and received my teacher license from PBA and then opened up my own full service salon called "The Kat's Meow". Jim still would come to visit me or we would meet in various locations for years to come. When I got my town home he came to visit Bianca and I again. She was three years old.

Another time we met in Cleveland when Jim was given a position as a "Special Teams Coach" with the Cleveland Browns, I took my mother my friend Lynn and her sister Turnup with me as a buffer. Jim took us all to diner at his hotel and at diner he asked Lynn to babysit Bianca so I could go back to LA with him for a while. I told Lynn to tell him that she had plans so I would have an excuse not to go. I would always love Jim, but loving Bianca more probably saved my life. I now learned to not even put the love of my children before the Lord! I would see Jim off and on most of my adult life , even after we had both had married other people. We would never sleep together, but we would still see one another. I knew if I did that would somehow make Jim think in his mind that I did that to him. The last time we were together I was 38. I made a life time of decisions based around not going back to Jim, even if they were wrong like marrying a man who I didn't love, in order to keep me from going back. I paid the price for that. I made an angry man out of my ex-husband. My guilt lead me give him everything that he asked for in our divorce, and I even allowed my ex-husband treat me bad during our divorce out of guilt I had for not loving him. I am currently working on healing from my mistakes. One thing that I know you won't get through this life without tribulations, however I was determined not to put my children in harms way and to make a good life for them. And now that they are both older and both in college it is now time for me and the purpose God Has for my life, I some times wonder what would have happened had I stayed with Jim?! I knew the truth about the love that we shared, but it was a worldly kind without Jesus at the center. And the lesson in it for me is that God allow it all to take place and like Paul, God left a thorn in my side so that I wouldn't go back. He said that He is a jealous God and to never put any gods before Him, and I did that with Jim, and now that God is first in my life, just maybe He will be gracious to allow me to have the kind of love He desires for me. Even now, it was difficult to include every moment of every day that we shared together. Maybe that was why Jim said to me that that anyone who writes a story of their lives generally aren't good, because I know it isn't humanly possible to fit it all in, but what ever the case, this chapter is clearly over and I look forward to what God has for me...

Made in the USA
Middletown, DE
04 August 2017